Grace Exceedingly Sufficient

Grace Equals God's POWER To Deliver You Completely!

Rudi Louw

Copyright © 2013, Rudi Louw Publishing

All rights reserved solely by the author. No part of this book may be reproduced in any form without the permission of the author.

Most Scripture quotations are taken from the *Revised Standard Version*, Holy Bible, Thomas Nelson Publishers. Copyright © 1983 by Thomas Nelson, Inc.

Some Scripture quotations were taken from the *New King James Version*, Holy Bible, Thomas Nelson Publishers. Copyright © 1983 by Thomas Nelson, Inc.

All Scripture quotations not taken from the RSV, NKJV and the Mirror Bible are a literal translation of the Scriptures.

The Holy Scriptures are just that, HOLY. Statements enclosed in brackets were inserted into Scripture quotations to add emphasis or clarify the meaning of what is being said in those scriptures. The integrity of God's Word to Man was not compromised in any way. Due care and diligence was cautiously exercised to keep the Word of Truth intact.

For example, the apostle Paul said in his second letter to Timothy in chapter three verse sixteen that:

"All Scripture is given by inspiration of God (literally God breathed) *and is profitable for doctrine, for reproof, for correction, for instruction **in righteousness**,"* NKJV

Table of Contents

The Marvel of the Holy Bible 5

Acknowledgments 11

Foreword 13

1. *God's Commission Upon Our Lives* .. 19
2. *By the Grace of God I am WHAT I am!* 27
3. *The Reign of Sin* 39
4. *The Free Gift and Its Reign* 51
5. *What Shall Our Response Be?* 81
6. *"Go and Sin No More"* 91
7. *Faith and Power* 109
8. *The Work of Redemption* 119

About the Author 131

The Marvel of the Holy Bible

1. Uninterrupted Theme and Inspired Thought

It took *1,500 years* to compile the Holy Bible, involving *more than 40 different authors*. Yet the theme and inspired thought of Scripture continues *uninterrupted* from author to author, from beginning till end.

2. Absence of Mythical Stories

Compare philosophies and theories about creation in the Middle East, Europe, Asia, Africa, and Latin America and you'll find mythical scenarios: gods feuding and cutting up other gods to form the heavens and the earth, etc.

In ancient Greek mythology, the Greeks see Atlas carrying the earth on his shoulders. In India, Hindus believe eight elephants carry the earth on their backs.

But in contrast, Job, the oldest book in the Holy Bible, declares that, *"God suspends the earth on nothing."(Job 26:7)*

This was said millennia before Isaac Newton discovered the invisible laws of gravity that delicately balance every planet and sun in its individual circuit.

Contrary to every other ancient attempt to give a creation account, *the Holy Bible pictures the creation of the earth in a very scientific manner.*

For example, in Genesis Chapter One, the continents are lifted from the seas, then vegetation is formed and later animal life, all reproducing *'according to its own kind',* **thus recognizing the fixed genetic laws.** In addition, we have the bringing forth of man and woman, *all done by God in a dignified and proper manner, without mythological adornments.*

The balance or remainder of the Holy Bible follows suit.

The narratives are **true historical documents,** *faithfully reflecting society and culture* **as history and archaeology would discover them thousands of years later. Not only is the Holy Bible historically accurate, it is also reliable when it deals with scientifically proven subjects.** It was never intended to be a textbook on history, science, mathematics, or medicine. *However, when its writers touch on these subjects,* **they often state facts that scientific advancement would not reveal, or even consider, until thousands of years later.**

While many have doubted the accuracy of the Holy Bible, time and continued research have consistently demonstrated that the Word of God is better informed than its critics.

3. Intactness

Of all the ancient works of substantial size, the Holy Bible survives intact, against all odds and expectations.

Compared with other ancient writings, the Holy Bible has more manuscripts as evidence to support it than any ten pieces of classical literature combined!

The plays of William Shakespeare, for instance, were written about four hundred years ago, after the invention of the printing press. Many of his original writings and words have been lost in numerous sections, *yet the Holy Bible's uncanny preservation has weathered thousands of years of wars, contradictions, persecutions, fires and invasions.*

Through the centuries Jewish scribes have preserved the Holy Bible's Old Covenant text, **such as no other manuscripts have ever been preserved. They kept tabs on every letter, syllable, word and paragraph.** *They continued from generation to generation to appoint and train special groups of men within their culture* **whose sole duty it was to**

preserve and transmit these documents <u>with perfect accuracy and fidelity</u>.

Who ever bothered to count the letters, syllables, or words of Plato, Aristotle, or Seneca for that matter?

When it comes to the New Testament, the actual number of preserved manuscripts is so great that it becomes overwhelming. ***There are more than 5,680 Greek manuscripts, more than 10,000 Latin Vulgate manuscripts and at least 9,300 other versions. Further still, there exists an additional 25,000 manuscript copies of portions of the New Testament.*** **No other document of antiquity even begins to approach such numbers.**

The closest in comparison is Homer's <u>Iliad</u>, with only 643 manuscripts. The first complete work of Homer only dates back to the 13th century.

4. Unmatched Accuracy in Predictive Foretelling

The Holy Bible is unmatched in accuracy in predictive foretelling. No other ancient work succeeds in this, or even begins to attempt this.

Other books such as the Koran, the Book of Mormon, and parts of the Veda claim divine inspiration; ***but none of these books contain predictive foretelling.***

This one undeniable fact we know for certain: *While microscopic scrutiny would show up the imperfections, blemishes, and defects of any work of Man, <u>it magnifies the beauties and perfection of God</u>. Just as every flower displays in accurate detail the reflection and perfection of beauty, <u>so does the Word of Truth when it is scrutinized</u>.*

Historian Philip Schaff wrote:

"Without money and weapons, Jesus the Christ conquered more millions than Alexander, Caesar, Mohammad, and Napoleon. Without science and learning, He (Jesus the Christ) shed more light on things human and divine than all philosophers and scholars combined. Without the eloquence of schools, He (Jesus the Christ) spoke such words of life as was never spoken before or since and produced effects which lie beyond the reach of orator or poet. Without writing a single line, He (Jesus the Christ) set more pens in motion and furnished themes for more sermons, orations, discussions, learned volumes, works of art, and songs of praise **than the whole army of great men of ancient and modern times combined**.*"* (*The Person of Christ*, p33. 1913)

Today, there are literally billions of Bibles in more than 2,000 languages.

Isn't it about time you find out what it really has to say?

Hey listen, the Holy Bible is all about Jesus, the Messiah, the Christ...

...*and everything about Jesus Christ is really about YOU!!*

Study Tips:

Read 2 Corinthians 5:14, 16, 18, 19, and 21.

In the light of these Scriptures, it should be obvious that, if you want to study the Holy Bible, *you should study it in the light of Mankind's redemption!*

Feed daily on **redemption realities** found in the book of Acts, in Romans Chapters One through Eight, and in Ephesians, Colossians, and Galatians, also in 1 Peter Chapter One, 2 Peter Chapter One, James Chapter 1, as well as in 1 and 2 Corinthians.

Acknowledgments

I want to acknowledge and thank one of my mentors in the faith, Francois du Toit, for blessing and impacting my life with revelation knowledge.

The portion on *"The marvel of the Holy Bible"* was borrowed from his website: http://www.mirrorword.net/ as students so often feel they have a right to do with things that come from teachers they respect. Just as Galatians 6:6 says: *"Let him who is taught the Word **share in all good things** with him who teaches."*

To all our dear friends and family, for all the love and support, and to Chase Aderhold and all those who helped me with this project:

THANK YOU!

Also, especially to my wife, Carmen;

For keeping me genuine by being my companion in life and partner in ministry,

I love and appreciate you so very much!

Foreword

Thank you for taking the time to read this book.

Let me start off by saying that *I am totally addicted to my Daddy's love for me.*

I am in love with Jesus Christ, *and that is enough for me!*

The love of God is so much more than a doctrine, a philosophy, or a theory. It is so much more and goes so much deeper than knowledge; it way surpasses knowledge.

We are talking heart language here.

I write *to impact people's hearts,* to make them see the mysteries that have been hidden in Father God's heart concerning Christ Jesus, and actually *concerning THEM,* so as to arrest their conscience with it, *that I may introduce them to their original design and to their true selves,* **and present them to themselves perfect in Christ Jesus** *and set them apart unto Him **in love**,* as a chaste virgin.

We are involved with the biggest romance of the ages!

Therefore this book cannot be read as you would a novel: *casually.* It is not a cleverly devised little myth or fable. **It contains** revelation into some things you may or may not have considered before.

It is the TRUTH of God, ultimate TRUTH, and therefore has direct bearing upon YOUR life. **The Word and the Spirit are my witness** *to the reality of these things!*

Be like the people of Berea whom the apostle Paul ministered to in Acts 17:11. Open yourself up to study the revelation contained in this book ***to discover for yourself the reality of these things****.*

Be forewarned! Do not become guilty of the sins of the Pharisees, ***or you too will miss out on the depth of fulfillment God Himself, who is LOVE, wants to give*** <u>***YOU***</u>.

Jesus said of the Pharisees and Sadducees that they strain out every little gnat BUT swallow whole camels. What He meant by that is that *some people seem to have it all together when it comes to doctrine and they love to argue.*

It makes them feel important, but it is nothing other than EMPTY religious and intellectual pride.

They know the Scriptures in and out, and YET they are still so IGNORANT about ***REAL TRUTH that is only found in LOVE.***

They are still so ignorant and indifferent ***towards the things that REALLY MATTER.***

They are always arguing over the use of *every little jot and tittle* and over the meaning and interpretation of *every word of Scripture.*

The exact thing they accuse everyone else of doing though, the precise thing they judge everyone else for, *they are actually doing themselves.* That is **they often downright misinterpret and twist what is being said, *making a big deal of insignificant things while obscuring or weakening God's real truth: the truth of His LOVE*.**

They are always majoring on minors <u>**because they do not understand the heart of God**</u> **and therefore they constantly miss the whole point of the message**.

Paul himself said it so beautifully,

*"…the letter kills but **the Spirit BRINGS LIFE**;"*

*"…<u>knowledge puffs up</u>, but **LOVE EDIFIES**."*

I say again:

Allow yourself to get caught up in the revelation I am about to share.

Open yourself up to study the insight contained in this book, *not only with a desire to gain knowledge, but also with anticipation* **to hear from Father God yourself; to encounter Him through His Word, and to embrace truth, in order to know and believe the LOVE God has for <u>you</u>**, *so that you may get so caught up* *in it,* ***that you too may receive from Him LOVES' impartation of LIFE.***

This revelation contains within it the voice and call of LOVE Himself to every human being on the face of this earth. *If you take heed to it, and yield yourself fully to it,* ***it is custom designed and guaranteed to forever alter and enrich your life!***

"If,
because of
one Man
(Adam's) trespass,
death reigned

through *(as a result of)*
that one Man,

MUCH MORE
will
those who receive
<u>the *abundance of grace*</u>
<u>and the *free gift* of</u>
<u>righteousness</u>
reign in life

through *(because of: as a result of)*

the one Man Jesus Christ."

~ Romans 5:17

Chapter 1

God's Commission Upon Our Lives

I believe that the greatest need for every single individual is to discover his or her full potential, *as revealed in Jesus Christ.*

If we look at the extent of sin in the world today and we see the real mess that we find ourselves in because of it, it is easy for us to begin to think, *'God, where is the witness you have brought forth in Your "Church"?'*

Especially in the light of Matthew's gospel where Jesus said of his disciples,

"You are the light of the world."

And, *"…you are the salt of the earth."'*

When we look at His disciples today, we can begin to question, *'Jesus, did you not perhaps expect too much of Your "Church"?' 'Did you not perhaps place too large a commission upon your "Church"?*

'I mean, just look at the meager effects of righteousness, and then look at the overwhelming effects of sin in the earth today.'

Listen; **God can not be blamed for this!**

If the *"Church,"* taken captive by the man-made Christian religion of today, could just discover *what God has intended to do through them all along,* **then and only then can the *"Church"* be what He has called them to be!**

The word that is translated *'Church',* is actually the word EKKLESIA in the original language. ***It refers to so much more than a building or an organization.*** It is meant to be used when referring to *all those who associate with Jesus Christ as individuals and as a whole.* It is also used when referring to *a smaller group of believers or followers of Jesus Christ who choose to fellowship together in friendship and relationship.*

The word EKKLESIA in the Greek is made up of two words: EK and KLESIA.

EK is a preposition **always denoting origin or source.**

KLESIA comes from the root word KALEO which means: *To call, to surname, or to summon by name.* It speaks of *an urgent invitation and implies and indicates* **the giving of a name to, or the receiving of the name of.** It also means: *To call or salute* **by name,** *to accurately identify by name, and* **to be assigned an identity.** It has to do with **being known by a specific identity,** in other words: *To call or salute* **by one's authentic name or original identity.**

In Matthew 16:13 and 16-18, Jesus reveals to Simon *the original design and purpose of **the son of Man.***

It was in the context of this revelation ***of Man's true identity revealed by God Himself*** that Jesus said He would **build** or **assemble** His "EKKLESIA;" His *"Church;"* **His BODY of BELIEVERS:** ***Those who know and understand their original identity, their joint-sonship with Him, based upon their true origin in Him, and therefore embrace their oneness with Him, and His indwelling!***

Jesus then went on to say that the gates of HADES from the Greek words, HA and IDEIS, literally meaning: ***not to see (referring to ignorance),*** **shall not prevail against** His EKKLESIA.

In other words: *That ignorance, that blindness, the spiritual forces of darkness, the prince of the power of the air; that confusion, that darkened understanding, which has blinded Men's minds to their true identity, and kept them in a cloud of deception concerning their original design and purpose,* ***shall not prevail!***

That which has kept people in bondage; that which has kept them in sin and kept them bound to a natural, fleshly-identity and opinion of themselves, and of others, and of God, ***shall not prevail!***

That which has kept people from seeing God's original design, the true identity of,

and purpose for, the human race, for every single individual, <u>as it was revealed in Jesus Christ</u> shall not prevail against the voice of the EKKLESIA!

The Church is the voice of TRUTH, the voice of those who do see these things; those who do see God's original design for Man, and Man's true identity, and God's purpose for the human race, *exactly as it all was revealed in Jesus Christ.*

The *'Church',* or EKKLESIA, therefore, *as those who associate with Jesus Christ as individuals and as a whole, followers of Jesus Christ, His disciples, as a body of believers* **are supposed to be BELIEVERS who have discovered and now understand <u>God's original design</u> of them and of all Men.** *They are supposed to understand God's eternal TRUTH about Man's true identity and value, and about His purpose concerning Mankind <u>as it was revealed</u> when God's Word became flesh in Jesus Christ.*

In Jesus Christ, *our original design, that image and likeness of God in which we are made, our true identity, our authentic real identity* **was revealed and put on display and then redeemed.**

Now, I believe that part of the secret to that discovery of that design and identity and purpose, which the *"Church",* the followers and disciples of Jesus Christ; **those who**

associate with what is revealed in Him, *needs to come to,* is to be found in Philemon 1:6.

Paul is writing this letter to a little *"house church."* So let's just read from verse 1 to follow the content of this conversation.

Philemon 1:1-6,

1 *"Paul, a prisoner for Christ Jesus, and Timothy our brother,"*

2 *"To Philemon our beloved fellow worker and Apphia our sister and Archippus our fellow soldier,* **and the church in your house***:"*

3 *"Grace to you and peace from God our Father and the Lord Jesus Christ."*

4 *"I thank my God always when I remember you in my prayers,"*

5 *"…because I hear of your love and of the faith which you have towards the Lord Jesus and towards all the saints..."*

It's one thing to have and exercise love and faith towards the Lord Jesus while *ignoring the saints.* But I believe the New Covenant we have entered into *does not allow room for that.* The same attitude that I express in worship towards my Father, as well as the love that I express towards Jesus, *is the same love that God desires for me to share and communicate in reality towards all Men, especially towards the brethren, my fellow lovers and followers of Jesus Christ.*

And now He says here in verse 6,

6 *"I pray that the sharing of your faith..."*

The Greek word for the word *"sharing"* used here is the word KOINONIA. It better translates as, *'fellowship'* in the English language.

In other words,

"...I pray that the fellowship – the communication of your faith..."

I like also the Afrikaans translation here. Directly translated into the English it speaks of, *"...the intimate **community forming** of your faith."*

In other words, Paul was saying here in verse 6,

6 *"I desire that your sharing; your communication; your fellowship; your KOINONIA; your intimate community forming together in the faith ...may promote the knowledge of all the good that is ours in Christ Jesus* (all the good **that is already in us** in our union with Christ Jesus)."

It's one of my favorite scriptures in the Bible, because I believe that linked to this desire and prayer of Paul, *is the heart that Paul and*

Father God both share for all of Mankind, and it's especially true for the body of Christ.

Their heart is for us to discover **every good thing that is already in us, every good thing** that has become ours in our understanding and insight into *the knowledge of* Christ Jesus.

Paul realizes that there is *such a vast treasure* **available and already given** to all Mankind, and especially the believer, **to enjoy.** But he also realizes that that treasure **needs to be communicated,** *in order that there would be **a promotion** of **all the good** that is ours as revealed and restored to us in Christ Jesus.*

Paul realizes that there needs to be **a promotion** of <u>all the good</u> **that is in us.**

And so allow me to communicate and promote to you **that treasure that is already <u>fully ours</u> in Christ Jesus, and which is therefore <u>in us already</u>.**

Chapter 2

By the Grace of God <u>I am</u> WHAT I am!

Turn with me to 1 Corinthians 15:10,

10. *"…but by the grace of God I am what I am…"*

Now Paul is not writing that as an excuse to his failures. He is not making an excuse and trying to apologize for a weak effort as a believer. No, He is glorifying and boasting *in the grace of God!*

He says,

"…by the grace of God I am WHAT I am…"

In other words,

'I'm not a failure; I'm not a weakling…'

So, just to be clear, *'I'm not perfect, just forgiven…'* or, *'I constantly fail,'* **was NOT what he was saying!**

As believers, **we need to discover ourselves, our true identity,** just like Paul did, **in Christ Jesus.** We need to discover ourselves **in the light of God's purpose for us.**

In that second half of verse 10, Paul goes on to say this:

*"...and His grace towards me **was not in vain**..."*

At the end of Paul's ministry he says,

"...I have finished the course..."

In Galatians 2:21 Paul says,

*"...**I did not frustrate** the grace of God..."*

In other words: **"I did not ignore that grace or put it aside. I didn't try and do it in my own steam and in my own energy; in my own ability and my own strength."**

In Philippians 3:3 Paul says,

*"...I put **no confidence** in the flesh..."*

And I believe that perhaps the biggest reason for the failure of the man-made version of Christianity, this Christian religion that has taken God's *"Church"* captive *from being the witness that it's called to be in this generation* **is because of its emphasis on the confidence of the flesh!**

I say again: **One of the biggest reasons for the failure of the man-made Christian religion, *to successfully impact this world*, is that, *they are always trying to promote***

the grace of God <u>with the efforts of the flesh</u>!

Paul says, *"…I put **NO confidence** in the flesh; but **I am WHAT I am BY THE GRACE OF GOD** …and His grace towards me **was not in vain**..."*

God's grace on your behalf, His grace towards you in Christ Jesus **is the greatest factor in your life!**

What do I mean?

I mean **what He has revealed concerning you there, in the grace of God,** and what He has done for you **there, in the grace of God,** is of the utmost importance, because **there is no other greater *reality* about you!**

God's grace towards Man is the greatest reality of our existence, *because it has everything to do with our original design, our true identity revealed and restored to us, in Christ Jesus, by that grace of God,* and therefore God's grace towards Man is of the greatest importance in this life!

Paul says:

*"…His grace towards me **was not in vain**…"*

In 2 Corinthians 9:8 the King James Version says that,

*"…God is able to make **all grace abound towards you**…"*

In other words: God has the ability to make **the full potential of His grace,** *the fullness of what He has made available to you, of what He has given to you in Christ Jesus,* **He is able to make it yours**, *in reality and in abundance, and in full measure and in overflow. He's able **to make it your portion; your inheritance.** He is able to cause you **to inherit it <u>fully</u>!***

*Listen God has **the ability to do that,** but even more, He desires to let His grace be **YOUR PORTION, in abundance!***

I know the enemy would seek, with all his might, *to again depreciate the grace of God,* so that we end up in this whole *Christian religious thing,* and it becomes *an effort of the flesh,* where we begin to *boast in the flesh again* and *put confidence* in the flesh again.

I believe God is challenging us in this day to re-examine and think long and clear about this:

What do we rely on? On what do we build our confidence?

God wants us to know that the grace demonstrated, shown, and given to us, by God Himself, in Jesus Christ; that grace of Christ Jesus towards us, **<u>is</u> the foundation for true confidence as Christians.**

If your confidence is related, *just in the slightest little bit,* **to who you are in the flesh:** where you come from, what kind of education you have, how strong you feel you are in your own talent and personality, or what you own and what you have achieved, *then you see, the enemy would be able to come in and* **challenge your confidence.**

But, if **I am <u>what I am</u> *by the grace of God*,** then the enemy loses his ground to operate from.

They challenged John the Baptist in John Chapter 1,

"What do you say about yourself?"

He says,

"I am what I am."

He says,

"…I am what the Scriptures say I am."

He says,

"…I am a voice crying in the wilderness."

"…I am, as it is written of me according to the Scriptures."

He says,

"…I am an expression of those Scriptures."

"…I am an extension of the Word."

"…I am a product of the Word."

He says,

"…I am a voice crying in the wilderness."

"…I am the very voice of the Scriptures."

"…I am amplifying the Word in the wilderness."

He says,

"…I have my identity; I have my confidence …my knowledge of who I truly am, in the very Scriptures themselves."

He says,

"…I am the very product of the word itself."

"…I come from the Word Himself."

Ephesians 1:3-7,

3 *"Blessed be the God and Father of our Lord Jesus Christ, who **has** bless**ed** us in Christ Jesus,"*

*"…with **every spiritual blessing** in the heavenly places (in the spirit realm; in the unseen realm of spirit-realities)."*

If verse 3 can genuinely become **your faith and your confession**, then you've truly **gained** something!

But so often our prayer is ***towards*** verse 3. We're praying **for** the blessing of God **to come.** We're praying **for** His grace **to come.** But if we can only **REALIZE** that He ***has* bless-*ed* us (already)** in Christ Jesus, **with *every* spirit-blessing** in the heavenly realm, in the spirit realm, the unseen realm of *spirit-reality,* then ***a new confidence will be birthed within us,* a new reality of who we really are will come into our spirit.**

Ephesians 1:4-6,

4 *"…even as He chose us* (associated us) *in Him, before the foundation* (before the KATABALO - before *the fall*) *of the world, that we should be holy and blameless before Him **in love**."*

5 *"He destined us **in love** to be His sons, through Jesus Christ, according to the purpose of His will,"*

6 *"…to the praise of His glorious grace, **which He freely bestowed on us** in the Beloved."*

I like that phrase, *"…to the praise of His glorious grace…"*

The word *"praise"* used here means: ***evaluation*. God wants my whole life *to be an expression, an evaluation of* (an estimation of; an adding value to) *His glorious grace towards me.*** God wants me to show, *in the way I live,* **that His grace towards me was not in vain,** that He didn't just hit the air, that He did not miss it with *me*. Amen!

I believe that if we, as individuals and corporately as the *"Church",* could *discover* **the full potential of what is involved in the grace of God, *in that redemption work of Christ Jesus,*** we would all realize that God *can* count on us and that He *is* counting on us. We would all realize that the commission, not just to the early believers, *but to us as well, is indeed **to go into all the earth <u>and proclaim the true gospel</u>** and **be*** the salt of the earth and ***be*** the light of the whole world.

Yes, we are all commissioned with that same commission, and we can do it too, because God doesn't count *on the ability of the flesh.* He knows our frame, He knows that we are but dust, *but He is not counting on the dust part of us,* **He is counting on the treasure we carry within** this frail, earthen vessel. And **that treasure, to its full dimension, *is available, to everyone who believes,* through the grace of God.**

Okay, now where was I?

Oh yes, Ephesians 1:6,

6 *"...to the praise of His glorious grace"*

God wants my Life to become *a praise song,* **to become a song *of appreciation* to the grace of God; *His glorious grace!***

7. *"In Him we have…"*

Not, *in Him we* **hope to have, or,** *in Him* **we are praying to have.**

No, *"In Him* **we have** *redemption…"*

You see, the so-called *"Church",* the fake one, the man-made Christian religion, ***is always caught up in the frustration of wanting to get somewhere in prayer, in worship, in practically everything they do!***

Because of this *deception,* they end up in this exhausting, never ending cycle of always having to go through *some kind of religious ritual,* to try and achieve *more,* to try and achieve *a greater breakthrough;* always trying to earn and achieve *more power, more glory, more blessing.*

When we begin to *discover what we all ALREADY HAVE* in Christ Jesus, then and then only, *do we begin to discover <u>a new foundation</u> to live from; a new strength and ability that is not of our own making!*

He says here in verse 7,

"In Him **we have** *redemption through His blood…"*

We are not trying to work ***towards*** salvation!

We are not trying to work ***towards*** some favor that we could possibly get from God!

No, **_we have_ all these things _already,_ because _we already_ have <u>redemption</u> through His blood.**

Ephesians 1:7-8

*"In Him **we have redemption** through His blood, **the forgiveness of our trespasses;**"*

*"...**according to the riches of His grace;**"*

*"...**which He <u>lavished upon us</u>!**"*

I have news for you, God's not handing out *a little bit of grace* here and *a little bit of grace* there, you know, so that *you* have the grace for this and *I* have a little bit of grace for that!

No, Ephesians 4:7 makes it clear that **God had but one measure whereby His grace *given to us* can be measured.**

Listen; **God's measure** is not ***your capacity!***

...Although, *your capacity* does have something to do with *your accommodation* and *your experience of* God's grace, that is true, **but let me tell you something: *God's measure is not limited* to Man's capacity to enjoy Him.**

Ephesians 4:7 says,

*"Grace was given **to each one of us;**"* (...to every individual on the face of this planet), *"...**according to the measure of Christ's gift**..."*

Can you see that, *"…Christ's gift,"* or, *"…the gift of Christ,"* **is the measure of God's grace towards Man?!**

That's the precise measure that He desires to *"...***lavish upon us!***"*

You might be sitting there, reading this book, and feel all inferior, and miserable, and *'I can't do it,'* or *'I failed in the past,'* or *'I failed this last week; yesterday even,'* and *'I suppose I'll fail again tomorrow,'* **and the enemy tries to condemn you with all kinds of feelings of guilt, and shame, and inferiority. But listen, the Word of God, the truth of the gospel wants to break through all that because God wants to lavish <u>you</u> with His grace.**

God desires *the power of the gospel, the power of His grace* **to abound, towards YOU!** He desires **His strong grace, His strong love** *to totally overpower you,* **to completely overwhelm you. He desires for you to be totally overwhelmed by His grace, by the content of His heart, and by the content of redemption, by the enormity of His love for <u>you</u>, and by His power towards <u>you</u> because of it!**

You see, when ***this reality;*** the reality of *the overflow of His love, the wealth, the abundance of it, the volume* of His grace, breaks through *in my heart,* **then something happens within you, something happens within your spirit; within your whole heart**

and soul ...*and even your body becomes affected by it!*

Hallelujah!

Proverbs 4:20-23 testifies, and bears witness to this reality:

"My son, be attentive to My Word (To the word of His grace; to the truth of the gospel); *incline your ear to what I am saying."*

"Let it not escape from your focus; (hold on to your insight into what I am saying) *keep the truth of my Word within your heart."*

"For that insight, (that truth of the gospel) **is life to those who find it, and healing to all their flesh!***"*

"Keep your heart with all vigilance (Guard the environment within your heart tenaciously; hold on to your insight gained, and vigilantly maintain your persuasion in these things; in the truth of the gospel, in what I am saying to you in Christ Jesus, in what I am saying to you in My grace towards you); *for from it* (from out of your heart, from out of your inner-most being, from that truth, from that insight gained, and from that conviction and persuasion maintained) *flow the springs of life!"*

But let's move on, I want to get to the book of Romans...

Chapter 3

The Reign of Sin

Turn with me to Romans Chapter 5 and let's start reading there in verse 12,

*"Therefore, <u>just as</u> **sin came into the world** through one man, and death, through sin, **<u>that death</u> spread to all Men, <u>as</u> all Men sinned**."*

That is quite an accurate summary of the extent of things, *the condition we find this world in today,* wouldn't you say?

The scriptures say elsewhere that *sin is a violation of the law.* I am not going to go into much detail here, but I think it is necessary and quite vital for us to establish *what that law was that was violated here.*

What was it that Adam violated?

It was his identity. It was the law of identity, it was the law of truth, the law of liberty; in other words: **What Father God knew to be true of Man.** Adam violated that *and so his liberty was on the line.*

Once you violate your identity <u>you inevitably lose your true liberty</u>! And thus, you become a slave to self-destruction.

Once you lose sight of the truth; <u>*God's truth*</u> (What God knows to be true about you, about your true origin; your true design, and therefore your true identity) *...once you lose sight of <u>that truth; God's truth about you,</u>* **then your purpose gets all messed up,** *and you totally miss it in life.*

<u>That death</u>, that missing it in life, *<u>that missing the mark</u> becomes a strong, invisible force within you that keeps you in bondage.* **You develop an assumed, false identity and purpose for living.** *That false identity* **is the fruit of deception,** <u>*and it is missing the mark*</u>. **Which Mark? The mark** *of your original design.*

Sin (HAMARTIA in the Greek is made up of HA and MEROS. HA is used as a presupposition to speak of something in the negative. Thus in this case, the negative form of MEROS meaning: **That which has merit, or, that which is inherently valuable, or has authentic worth.** MEROS speaks of something's **true merit.** Thus, to use the word HAMARTIA is to say that you are involving yourself with something that is **of no merit,** or of very little to **no value. You are moving away from that which has authentic worth, or true value, or merit. You are moving away from its true form, from its original design.**) Thus to SIN means: *to miss the mark – to live outside your true form, your design; your original, true, authentic design.*

Listen Sin and its consequences to your purpose *are nothing but the fruit of deception; the fruit of the influence of the father of lies.*

Adam was *led astray.*

He went astray *because he believed a lie.*

And so, because he believed the lie, ***therefore he no longer represented the truth; Man's original design, our true identity and purpose.***

Adam became slave *to a foreign identity.*

That foreign identity now expressed by Adam, *was the fruit of a lie, and the fruit of deception.*

The one who was supposed to lead the way went astray, **therefore we all drifted even further away from the truth.** We all lost our way. We were all led astray. **We all got hopelessly lost** *in our identity and our purpose.*

Romans 5:12-14,

12 *"…**that death** spread to all Men, **as** all Men sinned…"*

In other words, through one man's *violation of the truth,* **giving himself over** to Satan's *lies* …through one man's **self-deception,** through one man's **transgression** (of the law of original identity; authentic identity) ...through one man's *foolishness,* **all Men** (all of Mankind; the whole of humanity) **came into bondage ...and progressively so, more and more!**

13 *"Sin* (missing the mark – the mark of truth; the mark of our original authentic design; the mark of our true identity; THAT SIN...)

"...SIN (Living by a false identity, by a foreign identity; living outside our original design, THAT SIN) indeed was in the world, (even) *before the law* (...even before the Law of Moses) *was given,"*

"... **but sin is not (cannot be) <u>calculated</u> where there is no law (where there is very little to no truth whatsoever; where there is no accurate truth)**...*"*

The Scriptures make it clear that,

"...the law is **but a <u>shadow</u>***;"*

It's a mere representation of the truth, **simply a standard** *that spoke of* our true original design and purpose. **But the law wasn't that design and purpose in and of itself.** *It was merely a picture of it. The law was meant to serve as a mere reference. It merely implicated our original design and purpose. It indicated it, or referred to it, and pointed towards it. The law prophetically pointed to a greater reality that itself. It merely pointed to the image and likeness of God within us, to our*

original design and authentic identity, to our true design and purpose, to that which existed already, but was buried deep within us.

The Scripture states in John 1:17,

*"...the law was given through Moses, **<u>but</u> grace <u>and truth</u> came through Jesus Christ**."*

Thus, TRUTH didn't come through Moses. It didn't come through the law. The law was only a shadow of it, merely a shadow pointing to TRUTH, but truth finally came personally, it came in person. TRUTH came in Jesus Christ. TRUTH was revealed in Jesus Christ! (See also Hebrews 10:1)

So Romans 5:13,

13 *"…SIN indeed was in the world …even before the law* (**and even after the law was given**) *…sin indeed was in the world..."*

And I want us to notice the fact that, *just because sin could not be <u>calculated</u>,* ***it doesn't mean that sin wasn't there, that Sin wasn't in power.* It was in power**, amen?!

Just because sin could not be <u>calculated</u>, **it doesn't mean that sin wasn't there,** but rather that **S*in and its fruit of sin, weren't <u>recognized.</u>*** Sin wasn't <u>**known**</u>.

What Sin and its fruit of sin *left Man with* weren't <u>recognized.</u> **Our missing it in life,** *wasn't <u>exposed.</u>* **How empty, or, how far we were missing it, as far as the truth of our original design and purpose is concerned, as far as the truth of our original true identity is concerned** ...**how far we have missed it, as far as** <u>living *that* truth</u> **is concerned, and how empty we are because of it,** *wasn't exposed <u>to its full extent.</u> The power of sin, its influence in our lives, <u>wasn't exposed to its full extent</u>* **as long as there wasn't at least** *some resemblance of the truth.* **As long as there was** *no law, no standard of truth* **(however incomplete that standard and that truth might be)** *sin could not be known. Sin could not be known **outside of a measure**, it could not be calculated **outside of using at least some sort of measure, some sort of measuring instrument** ...**even if that measuring instrument fell short; <u>even if that measuring instrument, that measure, was only a shadow of original truth</u>**.*

Sin could not be calculated ***outside of that measure, outside of that measuring instrument,*** *in as much as you **cannot measure speed** without something to **calculate speed with.** You have to have **a realistic measure, a realistic measuring instrument.***

Listen it is impossible to calculate speed with a ruler. But, on the other hand also, *just* *because you have* **a somewhat adequate measuring instrument,** *it may still* **fall short in accuracy**. And that is exactly what the problem was with the law: **It fell short in accuracy,** and there it had to be done away with and **replaced with** *a greater, more accurate, measuring instrument.*

So, it was discovered that even the law **fell short,**

"...being **only a shadow** *of the good things to come…"*

*"…***only a shadow of that which is to come in Christ***,"*

*"…***only a shadow** *of the accuracy of truth* **to be revealed in Christ***,"*

A ruler may be adequate in measuring **short distances***, but* **it becomes inadequate** *if one wants to* **measure the distance between stars.** A ruler is an adequate measuring device, *only until one wants to measure in miles, or even worse, try measuring light-years,* **it is simply beyond a ruler's capability;** **it loses accuracy.**

You see, we were **blinded. We regressed into *living a lie.*** We regressed *into* **the depth of deception.** We regressed into *total* **ignorance.** We regressed into a **darkened understanding.** We regressed into **darkness.** We couldn't **see** *our sin.* We couldn't **see** *our blindness.* We couldn't **see** or **understand,** *we couldn't comprehend,* **the depth of it.** *It couldn't be* **calculated***; it couldn't be* **<u>fully</u> calculated***. We didn't even know what sin was, and we didn't understand, or fully know,* **the emptiness of sin;** ***the emptiness sin leaves us with,*** *until the law was given, until at least,* ***a <u>shadow</u>*** *of the truth, was revealed to us ...* **however incomplete and in many ways <u>inadequate</u>.**

So until the fullness of time would arrive, **until grace and accuracy of truth would come in Christ**, the law was given.

So, the law came, *to expose sin.*

13 *"…sin indeed was in the world, before the law was given,* **but sin could not be calculated** **(or understood).***"*

We were blinded to what it really was, *and* ***to what it actually left us with.***

14 *"…**<u>never the less</u> death**…"*

(Death speaks of separation. We are eternal spirit-beings. When someone dies they don't actually stop existing as a spirit-being, they are merely separated from this natural existence, and find themselves in another dimension of existence; a spirit-dimension. I used to have one kind of existence but now I have another kind of existence. I departed from my body, and I am now separated from the life I used to know. That is for the most part what death is all about, beyond the natural decay of that lifeless vacated body, which that person has now departed from. Thus death means: Separation. In this case it speaks of some sort of separation from God in relationship. No one can actually be separated from God altogether. God is everywhere. He upholds all of existence. He is existence itself. He gives to all, life, breath, and all other things. Thus we can never actually be separated from God, but we can exist in a separation of sorts, as far as our intimate relationship is concerned. There can be a disconnect form God as far as our mind-set and thought-process is concerned; *there can be a disconnect in our hearts.* So, this death, Paul is talking about, that death, *is a separation from God of sorts*)

Paul says,

14 *"...**never the less death**..."* (A separation from God: A separation from our true identity and purpose, from our sense of worth and value, from our place of belonging and connection with God)

*"...**yet death** (and all its destructive, negative forces; all its consequences)"*

*"...**yet**, death, **reigned**, from Adam till Moses..."*

That death: Living outside our original design; living outside of the life we were designed for, that death, **reigned**, its **effect** reigned, **its infection reigned.**

We were infected with its virus. It strongly affected us!

*"...it was firmly in place ...it was firmly established ...**its effects <u>reigned</u>**, you see ...**whether sin was recognized and understood or not, ITS EFFECTS <u>reigned</u>** from Adam to Moses."*

Now that was before the law, **<u>and afte</u>r the law was given.**

The end of its reign only came *when grace and truth came in Jesus Christ.* **The end of its reign came *in Christ's work of redemption!***

14 *"**Death (The fruit of Sin, the fruit of ignorance, the fruit of self-deception) <u>reigned</u>**, from Adam till Moses..."*

"...even over those whose sins were not like the transgression of Adam..."

Their sins are *the fruit of ignorance,* **inherited deception,** whereas Adam's sin was *the fruit of original self-deception.* Their sin cannot affect *the whole world,* **Adam's sin did!**

14 *"...for he* (Adam) *was **a type** of the one who was to come..."*

Adam was the father of all living; *the truth bearer* (Instead he became better known as *the lie bearer, or the sin bearer*). But he, in his role as: *Truth Bearer,* in his role as: *The father of all living* ...he Adam, in his role as:

The one who carries our original design, was only *a shadow, a type,* ***a copy****,* of the One who was to come: Jesus Christ.

Jesus Christ is *the original mold, the actual origin, the authentic original blueprint, the authentic original life of the ages, the true design, the true identity of the human race,* ***the true father of all living ...the original One ...the authentic Man ...the true TRUTH bearer.***

Chapter 4

The Free Gift and Its Reign

Romans 5:13-21,

13 *"…**yet**, death, **reigned**, from Adam till Moses …even over those whose sins were not like the transgression of Adam…"*

15 *"**BUT**…"*

In other words: *'What I want us to focus on **is not Adam**,' he says, '**BUT CHRIST!**'*

*"…**BUT** the free gift is **not** like the trespass…"*

That word *"like"* used here, in the original language, refers to like, **as in affect; or as in the effects of!**

*"…like **in affect** …like **in potential effects**."*

In plain English: **The effects of the Fall was negative, BUT the effects of the free gift was way more positive; it was far greater in it's affect!**

God wants us to discover **the full potential** that He placed **within the free gift,** because for so many years, the man-made Christian religious establishments just preached *sin* and almost nothing else. *They preached the fall of Adam, the sin-message and condemnation.* And their focus, under their own religion, has become so judgmental and so negative, and they have made so much of the devil, and therefore in their minds he has become so big and powerful, and all they can see and focus on is what the devil is doing on planet earth!

They say: *'look at this terrible, miserable tired old world we're living in. And the Devil is just doing more and more, bigger and bigger, worse and worse things on a daily basis now.'*

Let's rather stick to what Paul has to say; to what God through Paul has to say!

Verse 15,

*"**BUT** the free gift **is not** like the trespass…"*

It's not like it! It's not like the trespass in potential, its potential *is not like that of the trespass;* **its affect was MUCH GREATER, therefore its potential is MUCH GREATER!**

The gospel of Jesus Christ *is the proclamation of that **free gift!*** It's the proclamation of **the grace of God** *that **abounded** and **still abounds** towards all Men,* **in its full potential; its full power!**

And that's why that grace of God towards Man is therefore not an overdraft facility. It's not *just another excusing of our failings and*

our supposed weakness, our excuses. Paul wasn't making an excuse for his failings, and calling it weakness, when he said, *"…by the grace of God **I am what I am**."*

He wasn't saying, *'…by the grace of God go I.'* No, **He realized what was actually in that gift of grace.** He realized, not just the full potential, *but* **the merit** <u>that was his</u> in the *grace of God.* He realized that the effect of the free gift **was much greater** than the effect of the Fall. **If the Fall affected things, the free gift affected things in a far greater way!** He realized, **the merit** <u>that was ours</u> in the grace of God. He realized, not just the potential, *but* **the reality revealed,** *and therefore* **the actual power** <u>available</u> *in that grace.*

So he writes here in Romans 5:15,

*"…the free gift **<u>is not</u>** like the trespass **<u>for</u>**…"*

Now notice his argument here,

*"…**for** if the many* (all of Mankind) *died through one man's trespass, **much more**…"*

I want you to take hold of those two little words in your spirit!

*"…**much more**…"*

*"…**MUCH MORE** <u>have</u> the grace of God, and the free gift in the grace of that one man, Jesus Christ, <u>**abounded**</u> **to the many*** **(to the same many; to all of Mankind – it abounded for**

everyone; for every single individual on the face of the earth)..."

You see, *if you identify yourself as a believer today,* if you say, *'I'm a part of the body of Christ, a part of the "Church", a part of Jesus Christ,'* **then the commission that God placed upon His** *"Church,"* **He places upon you!**

And what is that commission? It is to be *a carrier of **the truth,*** to *be* the salt of the earth, to **be the light** of the world, which means that, your *witness...*

(A witness is someone who testifies in a court of law of what they've experienced, of what they've seen with their own eyes, *of what they know to be **reality,*** *of what they know to be **true***)

To **be** a witness, to **be** the salt of the earth, to **be** the light of the world, to **be** a carrier of ***the truth,*** means that your testimony ***to the reality of* LIFE,** *to **the reality <u>of that gift of LIFE</u>*** *in Christ Jesus,* **will have evidence. It will have impact!** It will sound forth from you and **it will have an impact!**

So don't let the enemy succeed in his efforts *to keep you inferior **by getting you to look at yourself and your own efforts in the flesh.***

Listen to that scripture again:

*"…**much more** have the grace of God …and the free gift in the grace of that one man, Jesus Christ, **abounded to YOU!**"*

The Scripture <u>does not say</u> that **God's effort** *to reconcile fallen Man to Himself and to introduce their original design, purpose, and true identity to them* **was a failure!**

The Scripture <u>does not say</u> that **God's effort was a failure!** And therefore <u>it does not even suggest</u> that now we still need all kinds of psychological helps to try and *solidify,* to try and *perfect,* the work of salvation Jesus Christ tried to accomplish through His blood, through that perfect display of His love for us, *but didn't quite succeed in.*

God wants to persuade us of our value and our worth to Him still!

God wants to persuade us about **the merit,** about**, the truth, the credit, the credibility and the value of** *His salvation!*

God wants to persuade every single one of us, even the law-minded, about **the merit** of the blood of Jesus Christ!

God wants to persuade us that, *"…where sin abounded **grace abounded all the more**!"* - Romans 5:20.

We as individuals **need to realize <u>*the reality*</u>** and <u>***the impact***</u> **of the abundance and <u>power</u> of God's grace towards us,** *so that we*

would no longer hang our heads in shame, saying in effect that, *'His grace towards me **is in vain!** I need something more to pick me up. I need a few more little habits of the flesh to lean on, you see, like little crutches. **I need a few more little sins in my life to fall back into,** because, you see, **God's grace is not quite making it with me** you know…'*

Romans 5:15-21,

15 *"…**much more <u>have</u>** the grace of God … **and <u>the</u> free gift** …**in the grace** of that one man, Jesus Christ, **ABOUNDED**…"*

Do you see here that, the grace of God, the grace of that one man, Jesus Christ, **embraces a gift?** Hallelujah!!!

You see, ***there is something inside the grace of God!***

The grace of God is not merely a nice little religious phrase. These truths are not just flowery little religious words.

The grace of God *involves the fullness of God's heart!*

Grace *contains everything God wants for Man, and wants to say to Man.*

The grace of God is everything God wants Man *to know,* everything God wants Man *to enjoy,* and everything God wants *to give us!*

That "*free gift*" that is contained in grace is referred to again there in verse 17 of Romans 5, and it's called: **The gift of righteousness.**

Righteousness is the gift contained in that grace of God. Righteousness is the heart of God for Man. It's the fullness of what God wants for us for us; *of what God wants us to enjoy!* **Righteousness is at the core of original truth, it's the core** *of our original design,* **it's at the core of what God** *knows to be the truth about Man.*

Righteousness is all about our true identity.

Thus, righteousness is the heart of God for us *and the gift given in grace!*

God desires for us to be so made right with Him; *to be so reconciled to Him.*

He desires for us to be so made right, to be so made whole; *to fully embrace <u>the truth</u> of our origin in Him and our design and our restoration to our true identity and our reconciliation to Him as Father, as Daddy, as the lover of our soul, as the One who is in love with us still!*

He wants us to fully embrace Him as the One we now are in love with, *because we have discovered that He first loved us!*

He wants us to fully embrace *such righteousness,* **to fully embrace** *such innocence,* **to fully embrace** *such oneness,*

such intimacy of fellowship with Him, that there would NO LONGER be ANY hint of suspicion in our mind and in our fellowship with Daddy God.

That's what that gift of God is all about.

The old English word Righteousness comes from the Latin: **right-wise-ness** – *to be wise to that which is right*. It's about **BEING** right. It means *to **be** right, accurate, or complete.* The Greek word used in the Scriptures is DICAROSONE, *which is really the context of the whole Bible.* In its most broken down form it means: ***Two parties finding likeness in one another.***

Thus righteousness is **the very foundation of** all friendship, *but especially **close intimate friendship**.*

How can two walk together **unless they are *agreed*,** unless they are ***compatible**? How can they walk together* unless they ***share an agreement**,* unless they ***agree together**?*

It's impossible to enjoy relationship if there is no common ground.

Righteousness defined, therefore, in the context of the Scriptures, means ***to be** totally restored to the Father –* <u>***to stand blameless***</u> ***before Him, with no memory of your past failures** – to stand before God* <u>***with a sense of being totally welcome***</u> *in His presence; because it's the presence of* <u>***your Daddy***</u>*.*

Thus righteousness means **to _be_ totally restored to the Father – _to stand blameless before Him_ – not just by the merits of the blood of Jesus alone, but also in all actuality because of Father God's love initiative, because of Daddy God's love for us demonstrated, _because of that original identity_ which that blood _redeemed and restored_!**

That gift: **Freedom from shame, our true identity restored, freedom from the power of sin itself, our original design re-awakened, our sonship, a reconciled relationship with Daddy God, RIGHTEOUSNESS.**

That gift *is gift-wrapped, it is all wrapped up in His love, it's gift-wrapped in the work of redemption; in the abundance of His grace.*

Romans 5:16 says,

*"And **the free gift is not like** the effects of that one man's sin…"*

Another translation says here, that,

*"…that gift of grace and righteousness, **have far more powerfully affected Mankind,** than Adam's transgression…"*

Another translation says,

*"**Far greater, is the gift,** than was the transgression…"*

Yet another translation says,

*"**God's gift of grace is out of all proportion,** to Adam's wrongdoing."*

We were not merely given the right to free ourselves from guilty feelings; **we were <u>actually set free</u> from being guilty!**

We were given the right *to be free indeed!*

*We were given the right to be **free* from guilt itself, *free* from shame itself, *free* from the power of sin itself!**

That is part of what righteousness is all about!

And *that righteousness* was wrapped up in the abundance of His grace, in God's extravagant love for us demonstrated; it was gift-wrapped in the work of redemption *and <u>given to Mankind as a gift</u>!*

Let me say again: Righteousness means ***to be totally restored to Father God* with no memory of your past failures!**

Righteousness means **to stand before Father God *with a sense of being totally loved and welcome in the presence of your Daddy!***

Righteousness means **to stand *blameless* before Father God, to stand *<u>actually</u> blameless* before Him, before your Daddy who loves you with all His heart!**

Righteousness means **to stand _totally restored_, _free_ from shame, _free_ from inferiority, _free_ from guilt itself, and therefore _free_ from the feelings of guilt, and _free_ from insecurity,**

..._free_ **from weakness,**

..._free_ **from failure,**

..._free_ **from shortcomings,**

..._free_ **from the power of sin itself,**

..._no flaws,_

...**as _free_ as _free_ can be!**

Righteousness means **_we are restored to our original state_, _to what we were in the heart of God before the creation of the world even_, before the Fall ever happened!**

Righteousness means **_we are fully restored to our original design_, to _our original identity_ and to _our original purpose_,**

It means **_we are actually reconciled_,**

..._**actually restored**_,

..._**actually righteous**_,

...**no more excuses,**

...**as _free_ as _free_ can be!**

Do you think that, if the fullness of this revelation *were **to begin to burn in the hearts of the followers of Jesus, in the hearts of BELIEVERS**, do you think that **there would be any excuse left** for us as the living "Church" **to tolerate Satan's bondage in ourselves?***

Do you think that, if the fullness of this revelation *were **to begin to burn in our hearts, that there would be any excuse left for us** the living "Church" to allow the world **to continue in ignorance and darkness and deception** by the influence of that father of lies?*

I don't think so!

I believe that this is the revelation, **the revelation of righteousness *is the revelation* that will undo ignorance, it will undo confusion, it will undo lies and deception, *it will undo the devil's works!***

This revelation is the revelation *of a successful redemption!*

The revelation of a *successful redemption* *is* the revelation *that will cause such a revival, such a restoration, such a reformation to hit this earth like we have never ever seen before!*

For years I grew up thinking we had to pray for revival. I thought we had to fast longer, and pray more, and repent more, and wait longer. But I've discovered that the fullness of grace

has already been given *to each one of us.*
I've discovered that we no longer have to plead with God to tear open the heavens, **because *He already did so*, over two thousand years ago!**

And so you see now, if we continue to pray for and seek for some kind of revival, *we are going contrary to the revelation of the New Covenant.* We are, in effect, asking God *to repeat His work, to repeat what He has already made abundantly clear, to repeat the New Covenant established in His blood, as if God is a glutton for punishment!*

Listen; that my friend is an impossibility, *for He died once and for all, and He is not going to do it again!*

No persuasion will persuade the court of heaven to send the Son of God back into the pit again!

The work of redemption doesn't need to be repeated! *God was clear enough in the demonstration of His love for us the first time around!* He cannot prove it any stronger or demonstrate it any clearer!

I'm telling you, the *"Church"* as a whole *has no excuse for the ignorance that it walks in.*

God wants us to finally, and fully, wake up to *the reality* of the <u>abundance</u> of grace, *which is out of all proportion* to what happened in the Fall!

'But, brother, I'm so struggling to give up my smoking …and I'm struggling to get rid of this habit of pornography …and I'm struggling with my flesh and what not …and these addictions …and this homosexuality …don't you know I was born with this 'gift' …oops …I mean … this curse?'

Hey listen, *stop believing a <u>LIE</u>!*

Quit struggling with your struggling and get caught up in the abundance of His provision.

Quit struggling with your struggling and get caught up in the abundance of His grace!

The intensity of His love for you and therefore the abundance of His grace towards you *are <u>out of all proportion</u> to the power of the enemy!* It is <u>out of all proportion</u> to the weak effort of the enemy *to keep you bound up* in DECEPTION and in a LIE; in THE FLESH, and in SIN!

There is **much more power** in the gospel of Jesus Christ, ***in the truth*** *of redemption,* ***<u>to deliver</u>****, than there is in sin, to bind you up!*

If sin had some effect on Mankind, to keep people in bondage to *a false* identity, to a *fake* identity, to *alternative fulfillment*, to drugs and sex and greed and whatever, **God is saying to you**, that, **in His grace towards you, in the grace of Jesus Christ, *there is <u>such a tremendous power</u>* available to <u>YOU</u>!**

That power *comes to a release* when you take a hold of the truth of the gospel, *with conviction.*

God's power *comes to a release* when you take a hold of A SUCCESSFUL REDEMPTION, *with total conviction*, *with an aggression against sin in your spirit*, *with a heart that says,*

'God, inject my life with the revelation of these things; these REALITIES;'

'…inject my spirit with the revelation of the REALITY of righteousness.'

You see, we no longer have to work *towards* righteousness, and seek to *accomplish* righteousness *after the efforts of the flesh, and after some religious pattern.* **It's the free gift of God's grace to us!**

When we *believe* this, *we experience its reality!*

Peter and John looked at that man that was crippled from his birth. There was no hope for him, no hope for this man. Religion couldn't help him. Well, they could perhaps feed and clothe him, and provide some shelter for him to sleep in when it gets cold, or, *'we can persuade our government to use our collective tax dollars and make it as comfortable for you as possible,'* **but, that's as far as religion can go**. Noble, honorable, *perhaps,* it depends on which political views you hold… ha… ha…

ha… *'But, the effects of the curse in your person and in your body, sir, **there is just nothing much we can do about that!***'

Peter could have had the same kind of weak religious response,

'Hey listen man, let us put you in touch with our "church", and I'll tell you what, you go talk to the man called Stephen. He is one of our appointed deacons, and tell him you talked to us, and he will put you on the list of people in this community we are trying to help…'

But no, Peter didn't have that response. He looked at the man, intently, *and Peter **<u>knew</u>** that <u>what he had</u> in this gift of grace was an abundant measure.*

***He <u>knew</u> that* God had given *Himself* to us in that gift of grace.**

Peter <u>knew</u> that that water he was partaking of from heaven, was not just to quench his own thirst. It became within him *a fountain, an artesian spring, welling up, bubbling up, and springing forth, from within,* a fountain of living water, *of life giving water!* And he allowed that fountain *to burst forth towards this man* and he became *an extension of the grace of God, of the love of God, of the power of God towards this man,* he became *an extension of God Himself towards this man,* and he locked eyes and soul with this man.

He said,

"Look at us!"

"…__what we have__ we give unto you!"

Not *"…what we hope to have…"*

No!

"…what we have!"

"…__what we have__ we give unto you!"

God wants us, as His *"Church",* **as disciples and BELIEVERS, to discover** __what we have__ **in Christ Jesus, in the abundance of His grace, in that grace which is** __out of all proportion__ **to the effects of Adam's transgression, to** *the effects* **of** *the curse* **that entered this world!**

In our discovery of __what we have__ in Christ Jesus, **we will discover** *a new confidence, a new strength* **within our spirit.** *We will discover* why Paul could say,

*"**I'm not ashamed of the gospel of Jesus Christ. It is the very power of God unto salvation for everyone who believes it!**"* - Romans 1:16

Let's read Romans 5:16, again.

16 *"And **the free gift __is not__** like the effects of that one man's sin"*

"…for the judgment (...the fruit; the inevitable result, the natural consequences, the outcome), *that judgment following that one man's trespass, his sin, brought condemnation…"*

I'm so glad that the gospel of redemption deals with sin! It deals with both the condemnation *and the power* of sin.

Paul continues,

*"…but **the free gift**, following the many trespasses, **brings justification**…"*

It brings *acquittal!* It brings *innocence, real* innocence! It brings with it RIGHTEOUSNESS!

In the light of this, Romans 8:1 & 2 states,

1 *"**There is THEREFORE now** no condemnation for those who are in Christ Jesus,*

(…and we have just seen earlier in Romans 5 **how all Mankind is in Christ Jesus,** amen,)

2 *"For* (because) *the law* (the ruling, the verdict) *of the Spirit of life,* **(Mankind's redemption)** *in Christ Jesus, **has** set us free, from the law of sin and death* **(…from *the* effects of the Fall …from *the power* of sin and death)**…"

Because of **the reality** of these things Paul continues in Ephesians 4:17-24, and he says,

17 *"Now this I affirm and testify in the Lord, that,* **you must <u>no longer</u> …you no longer need to** *live as the Gentiles do* (as the world does …how do they live?), **in the futility of their minds;"**

18 *"…***they are darkened in their understanding,** <u>alienated from the life of God</u>**, because of the ignorance that is in them,** *due to the hardening of their hearts"*

They are darkened in their understanding, because of the ignorance that is in them.

None of this is God's fault!

They hardened their own hearts.

They are alienated from the life of God, not because God has alienated them, but because they have alienated themselves from it and from Him.

They are alienated from the life of God that is within them, they are alienated from God, because of the ignorance that reigns within their thinking!

They hardened their own hearts, that's why they have a darkened understanding!

(John 3:19 says,

*"And **this is the judgment**...* (It is not a judgment against Man placed upon them from God, no, it is a judgment Men has placed upon themselves.) **This is that judgment: Light has come into the world, <u>but</u> Men loved darkness rather than light…"*)

Ephesians 4:19 goes on to say,

19 *"…they have become callous, and* (therefore) *have <u>given themselves up</u> to licentiousness* (they have given themselves a license to sin), *greedy* (eager), <u>*to practice every kind of uncleanness*</u>*."*

But, verse 20 says,

20 **"You did not so learn Christ!"**

21 *"…assuming that you have heard about Him, and **were taught in Him, <u>as the truth is (revealed and established)</u>** *<u>**in Jesus**</u>*."*

22 *"Put off* (you are free now to put off) *your old man* (your old identity, your old mentality and tendencies) **which belongs to your former manner of life and is corrupt…"**

(How did that corruption take hold?

*"…**through <u>deceitful</u> lusts**…"*)

So, *"Put off your old man **which belongs to your former manner of life and is corrupt through <u>deceitful</u> lusts**,"*

23 *"…and **be renewed in the spirit** (the whole attitude) **of your minds** (instead),"*

24 *"…and put on the new man (your true identity …your original design …your true design and purpose)"*

*"…put on the NEW MAN **created after the likeness of God in righteousness and holiness of <u>the truth</u>**."*

Let's get back to Romans 5:17-21,

17 *"If, because of one man's trespass, his sin, death reigned, as a result of that one man, **much more will those** who receive…"*

Who are the *"**those**"* he is talking about? All of Mankind, everyone included in the work of redemption, in Jesus Christ's death and resurrection.

*"…much more will those **who receive** the abundance of grace and the free gift of righteousness **reign in life,** through the one man, Jesus Christ."*

You see, even though all Mankind, every individual (that includes me and you), even though we all had **the ability to rule and reign in life** over the law of sin and death, over the *power of* sin and death, over *the effects* of the Fall, even though we had that ability **restored back to us,** *there is something hugely crucial we must understand:* **The grace of God cannot operate automatically.** The grace of

God has to be *"**received,**" it has to be wholeheartedly embraced;* **it has to be believed!**

Listen; believing *is receiving!*

Redemption is a reality!

The grace of God was given!

And now God is waiting for *you!*

And here you are, waiting for Him to do something, **when the grace of God is given ALREADY!**

Believe *the reality* of redemption!

BELIEVE IT!

EMBRACE IT FULLY!

17 "…***much more* will** those who ***receive*** … ***those who believe*** …***reign in life***…"

That's not struggling through life!

"…***reign in life;***"

Can you picture the difference between struggling through life and **reigning through life?** That means when a situation would arise *that would normally get the better of you* and get you down, and depressed, and in the gutter, *then suddenly **you realize** that,*

*'Something is given to me, it is deposited in my spirit <u>already</u>, through the knowledge of Him I am fellowshipping with, and that something is called **revelation**. It's called **faith**, it's called **<u>God's power available</u> through the abundance of God's grace, it is God Himself available to me, availing Himself to me, and that puts me into a new position of strength.'*

All that is deposited within me, <u>through the truth</u>, and by the Spirit of truth, the Spirit of God, **that Spirit within me**, **puts me in a new position of strength because I'm now in <u>a new</u> relationship with God;** *a faith relationship.*

Therefore I'm now finding myself in <u>a new</u> relationship towards the problem, or the sickness, or the temptation, *and I change <u>my attitude</u> towards that thing!*

I'm <u>no longer intimidated</u> by the circumstance, or the disease, or the temptation, or the Devil himself, *but I can now* **speak from** *the throne room, from* **where I am seated** *with Christ Jesus,* **in** *and* **as** *the right hand of Father God,* **in union with God Himself!**

I'm in a place of authority. Out of my union with God, I share in God's executive authority and I can now **speak** and **declare** to that enemy, to all the forces coming against me, that **the One who lives in me,** the One I am now in **a new** relationship with, **a relationship of trust and faith, is worth my relying on** and that **the strength and power I draw from Him is out of all proportion** *to the strength, to the ability, of my enemy or circumstance to snare me and trap me in temptation and weakness and defeat!'*

For so long our attitude towards the strength of temptation and the strength of the enemy has been so negative, wringing our hands in fear and trepidation, and weakness!

'Oh, I hope I'm going to make it through today, because yesterday I failed and I suppose this is going to be another one of those miserable days. And I just don't know how I'm going to make it, and, Oh, Jesus, just come quickly, because if You don't come quickly, with a revival, or the rapture, or something …to, to, …to RESCUE me, I'm just going to slip up again, and I don't know how long before I backslide all together, or before I've sinned so much, that I can no longer make it into Heaven…'

And <u>in our attitude</u> towards temptation, *there has been a subtle introduction of deception* into the *"Church"*, *never mind the world,* where we just take for granted that we are not strong enough to defeat temptation!

*'We are just too weak, brother Rudi. No one can ever attain to that level of **consistent** freedom and victory over temptation.'*

'…oh, we are all but sinners …you know …the effects of the Fall, brother,'

And so we cling to our sin-nature teachings,

'…and it's our lot in life, brother …to fail in the flesh…'

And we go on accommodating sin in the flesh!

With such a sin-nature; or dual-nature teaching, **and such a rotten loser attitude, and the inevitable weakness it brings, no one can stand against temptation!**

But I have news for you from the Scriptures, from the Spirit of God Himself:

*"…**no temptation has overtaken you, against which He has not already made a way of escape,**"*

*"...**against which He has not already made provision for in His grace!**"*

There is a way of escape – **the provision has already been made!**

And that way of escape is not just running away and hiding either! That way of escape becomes available to you *when you come into agreement with the truth of God's word* **and you decide *against* that sickness or that temptation, or that sin you're in, or that circumstance,**

...and so then, you, *from the heart, for real,* <u>come against</u> that thing, with the whole attitude of your heart and mind, and you refuse to receive that thing, or embrace it and tolerate it within you and within your life, and *then* you enter into the victory, in the name of Jesus.

By *faith* in what is revealed in that work of redemption concerning you, and by fully trusting in God, who upholds His Word, you enter into that victory, *and thus that way of escape* <u>becomes available</u> *to you* <u>practically.</u>

And so that temptation or that sickness, or that sin, or that circumstance *loses its hold over you,* it loses its power, and you beat it!

Therefore, to summarize, you take on an attitude and confession **that comes from faith, and it says to that thing, '*I conquer you!*'**

It says,

'*I reign in life through Christ Jesus!*'

It says,

'I will no longer be dominated by these forces …by this circumstance …by this sin …by this sickness …by this fear …by this insecurity' ...or whatever might be coming against you!

So, you take on a faith attitude and a faith confession that comes from faith and it says,

'I will no longer be dominated by spiritual or physical poverty and lack …but in the name of Jesus I conquer you!'

'Because in Christ Jesus I am more than a conqueror, and I am not just speaking from my top six inches, from my mind and intellect, but I'm speaking from the abundance of truth living in my spirit that is alive in my heart, that I embrace fully and BELIEVE!'

That attitude and that confession that I take on **that comes from *faith* knows that *I've been released* into *righteousness*, because with my heart I believe the integrity of His word! And therefore I hold fast to the confession of my faith! And this confession is also made from my heart, from the faith that is alive there, about my salvation in the work of redemption! And I know** that, *"that confession is therefore made unto salvation!"* - Romans 10:6-13

So, I declare that, **'By the gift of Christ Jesus, and by the abundance of His grace** *that is towards me, by faith in it, <u>I am saved</u>!'*

With my heart I believe the integrity of His word of truth; the gospel of my salvation! **I know that it's <u>covenant</u> principle that I'm standing on! I'm not standing on some weak little human doctrine or some mere philosophy of Man's brilliant imagination! But I'm actually standing on <u>the integrity</u> of the heart of God and the work of God!'**

You see, God Himself is *the author of this gift, of this grace and truth* in this gift of Christ Jesus!

Through the revelation of the truth and through the revelation of the abundance of His grace, *God wants to do something in our spirits which will totally change our attitude towards sin and weakness!*

It will change our attitude towards any negative circumstance; *any negative thing!* It will change our attitude towards *the thief* that comes to steal, kill, and destroy, towards *the Devil* and all the forces of darkness!

And we'll no longer walk inferior to them, *but we'll walk superior to them, for we reign in life* because of Christ Jesus and in Christ Jesus and through Christ Jesus, abiding, by faith, *in the knowledge of our redemption,* and abiding in Him, *relying on Him,* trusting in Him *to empower us,* and to

uphold His work of redemption *with power* in our lives!

We put our trust *in Him!*

Romans 5:17-21 says that,

17 *"...because of, **as a result of**, that one man, **sin reigned, death reigned**..."*

BUT you see, **the gospel doesn't stop there in the middle of that sentence,** although unfortunately, for many many years the man-made Christian religious *"Church"* with their man-made religious beliefs has stopped reading there!

But look at what it continues to say,

*"...**much more** <u>will</u> those who receive ... those who believe ...those who embrace fully ...the abundance of grace, <u>lavished upon them</u>, in Christ Jesus, and the gift of righteousness that comes with it, **much more, because of these things, <u>will they</u>, and <u>do they</u>, reign in life!!**"*

He says, *"...**they will reign in life!**"* **Those who receive, those who BELIEVE these things, <u>they will reign in life</u>!** And **it is all ours,** *"...through the one man Jesus Christ!"*

Listen to the tenses now, used here in verse 18, the *"**then,**"* and the *"**so now**"* realities, **which show how drastically things have changed for us in Christ Jesus, and indeed**

for all Mankind, *but especially for those who BELIEVE* these things.

So, listen for the *"**then,**"* and the *"**so now**"* realities, here in verse 18,

18 *"**Then**, as one man's trespass led to condemnation for all Men, **so now**, one man's act of righteousness leads to **acquittal and life for all Men**."*

19 *"For, **(just) as**, by one man's disobedience* (ignoring of truth …ignoring of true spirit reality), *many* (the many, all Mankind, every single individual) *were made sinners;"*

*"…**(just) so**, by one man's obedience, the many* (the same many, all Mankind, every single individual) **will be** (**shall be**) ***made righteous**…* (**They actually are in reality made righteous** *by His act of obedience; by His work of redemption*)."

20 *"Where sin increased* (where sin *abounded*), *grace increased;* (**grace superseded**; grace *abounded*) ***all the more**,"*

21 *"…so that,* **(just) as** <u>sin reigned</u> *in death,* **grace** *also might* **(now) <u>reign, *through righteousness*</u>**,*"*

"…to (bear the fruit of) *eternal life* (that original design, that original life, the life of God, exhibiting His image and likeness and His rule and authority in human life), *through Jesus Christ our Lord."*

Chapter 5

What Shall Our Response Be?

Romans 6:1-23,

1 *"What shall our response be then? Are we to continue in sin that grace may increase?"*

Shall we just carelessly continue in sin so that grace will just have to continue to increase and abound?

2 *"**By no means!**"*

May it never be so! God forbids it!

"How can we who died to sin…"

(...in the death of Christ – *by us understanding what actually took place on that cross; what was so clearly revealed there*)

*"…How can **we who died to sin** still continue to live in it?"*

3 *"**Do you not know** that all of us…"*

(...all of Mankind – *but especially us who see and understand what actually took place and was so clearly revealed on the cross*)

3 *"**Do you not <u>know</u>** that all of us who have been immersed into Christ Jesus…"*

(…*by God's doing* – see 1 Corinthians 1:30, 2 Corinthians 5:14-21, and Ephesians 2:4-6)

3 *"**Do you not <u>know</u>** that …**we were immersed into His death?**"*

4 *"We were buried therefore with Him, by immersion* (by God's doing) *into death, so that,* **(just) as** *Christ was raised from the dead, by the glory of the Father,* **<u>we too</u> might** (now) **walk in newness of life**.*"*

5 *"For since we have been **united** with Him in a death like His…"*

We were **united** with Him in the type of death he died, **certain death** on the cross. **We were <u>united</u> with Him in the same death, <u>in His death</u>. We were absolutely united and totally immersed with Him in His death, therefore,**

*"…**we shall be** (we are in reality therefore also – we are <u>certainly</u>) **united with Him in a resurrection like His**.*"*

We are united in the same resurrection, *in His resurrection,* carrying <u>the same power and authority</u> in our lives, as it did in His, *to <u>separate us from our former life.</u>*

6 *"**We know** that our old self…"*

(...Our false identity, assumed through deception – an alternative identity, assumed from, and shaped by, and influenced through the father of lies);

6 *"**We know** that …**that old self** (**that old fallen identity**) **was thoroughly crucified with Him**,"*

"…so that the body of sin **(that old sinful person; that Sin - that old missing the mark identity; that old identity inherited through the Fall)** *might be destroyed* **(in His death)***,"*

"…and we might **(now)** *no longer be enslaved to sin."*

(...**enslaved to missing the mark, enslaved to living outside our original design, enslaved to living a lie. We are free! We are no longer enslaved to living an assumed false identity, living outside our true identity;** *our original identity as children of God and partakers of the Divine nature.*)

*"…We know that our old self **was crucified** with Him, so that the sinful body* (the totality of that natural identity; that fallen mindset) *might **be destroyed*** (in that crucifixion and death) *and **we** might **no longer** be enslaved to sin."*

7 *"For he who has died **IS freed from sin.**"*

8 *"**And since we have died with Christ, we believe it only logical that we shall also be***

(we have also now been) *made alive with Him* ...*in His resurrection.*"

A better translation reads that,

8 "*And since we have died with Christ, we believe it only logical that* ...*we were, at the same time, also made alive with Him in His resurrection.*"

9 "*We know that Christ being raised from the dead will never die again;* **death no longer has dominion over Him.**"

10 "*Therefore, the death He died He* **died to sin**, *once and* **for all**, *but the life He lives He lives to God.*"

11 "**Just so, likewise, you also,** **must CONSIDER**..."

(You must come to the correct, logical, mathematical CONCLUSION)

11 "**Just so, likewise, you also** ...*you must consider yourselves dead to sin and alive to God, in Christ Jesus, in His death and resurrection.*"

12 "**Let no sin, therefore, reign in your natural bodies, to make you obey its passions.**"

13 "**Do not yield your members to sin as instruments of Sin**,"

"…but instead, yield yourselves to God, as individuals <u>who have been brought back to life</u> from the dead,"

"…and so then, yield your members to God as instruments of righteousness."

14 *"<u>For sin will not have dominion over you</u>, since you are under grace,"*

(**You are under the influence of truth** *and therefore the power of grace*)

14 *"<u>For sin will not have dominion over you</u>,"*

"…since you are under grace, and no longer merely under law **(just ignorantly trying to follow some rules);**"

To be under grace means you are under the influence *of what God accomplished in Christ Jesus, in the work of redemption!* **It means you are under the influence of that work of grace** *because it is accurate truth!* **To be under grace means you are under the influence <u>of the accurate truth</u>** *of how God succeeded at setting us free in Christ and restoring us back to our original design and true identity;* **to righteousness, in the work of redemption.**

15 *"What then? Are we to sin because we are not under law but under grace?"*

"<u>By no means</u>!"

If you still reason this way, *you do not understand grace yet;* you do not understand *what grace is truly all about yet!*

Listen; if you are still living in sin, it is because *you do not yet grasp the real power of grace and truth!*

To be still attracted to sin *is to be ignorant of the appeal ...of the power of that grace and truth revealed* in the incarnation of Christ and the work of redemption!

The magnetic power of that truth revealed in redemption, *the magnetic power of grace, of the love of God **is much stronger** than the magnetic power of sin.* In fact it is **out of all proportion stronger** in its attraction; *its attractive powers.* It is **way more powerful** than sin's appeal. It's liberating voice is **much stronger** than the voice of sin!

In that incarnation *our original identity was revealed!* And in that work of grace and redemption *the truth of our original identity was affirmed!* In that work of grace and redemption, *we were restored to our original identity,* through the power of God; *through the grace of God!*

Hallelujah!

In that grace, in that incarnation and work of redemption <u>we were redeemed</u>, and therefore also restored to original, accurate

truth! *Because of the accuracy of that truth revealed and restored to us, it is out of all proportion more powerful than sin; just as much as truth is out of all proportion more powerful than a lie, or, just as much as light is out of all proportion more powerful than darkness.*

There is no comparison!

There is no competition either! Darkness is powerless against light! Light absorbs the darkness and turns it into light every time!

In the same way, accurate truth exposes and undoes the lie every time!

But Paul says, and now he interjects something equally important to realize, he says,

16 "*Do you not yet know that, if you yield yourselves to anyone as a willing and obedient slave…*"

"*…you are that ones slave?*"

"*…you are slaves of the one you obey;*"

"*…you are either slaves of sin, which spells death to you,*"

"*…or you are willingly obedient <u>to the truth</u> which is the essence of righteousness … and spells real freedom and life to you!*"

Then in verse 17 he continues and he says,

17 "**But I am so thankful to God, that though you <u>who were once</u> slaves of sin, you have now become obedient <u>from the heart</u>**..."

He is talking about the impact and influence of the love of God upon our hearts; **true love <u>from the heart</u>!** "*We love Him **because He first loved us**.*" - 1 John 4:19 But really he is referring to the obedience **of *faith*** here. Faith that is inspired by love (Galatians 5:6). Real faith that is ***from the heart***.

"...***you who <u>were once</u> slaves of sin, you have believed from the heart, <u>that standard of teaching</u>***..."

(...**you have believed the truth of what God accomplished in Christ Jesus, in His incarnation and His work of redemption,** *to restore us back to our original design by revealing and restoring our original identity and value to us.*)

"...***you have believed <u>from the heart</u>, that <u>standard of teaching</u> which was delivered to you***..."

Or, "***<u>by which you were delivered</u>***" when you became committed to it, when you believed it and embraced it fully.

18 "...***and, <u>having therefore been set free from sin</u>, you have become willing slaves of righteousness***..."

(...**you have become willing slaves of accurate truth, of a life that fully reflects and exhibits your true identity and original design as sons of God, revealing and radiating your origin. He is your origin; You are Love's own image and likeness!**)

19 *"So, allow me to just clarify one more time, and let me speak in down to earth human terms,"*

*"...**because of the limitations and restrictions of Man's natural thinking**."*

"I am saying that,"

*"...**<u>Just as you once yielded</u> your members** (your mind and body) **to impurity and therefore to greater and greater iniquity,"**

*"...**<u>so now, in the same way, yield</u> your members** (your mind and body) **to that righteousness restored to you, for sanctification's sake."***

(...**so that it may cleanse you, change your life, and set you free from the influence of your former false identity. So it may deliver you from sin, from incorrect and harmful thinking and from the actions that follow as a result of that old mindset.**)

20 *"**When you were slaves of sin, you were totally free from any thinking that related to righteousness**"* You gave righteousness no thought; *you gave it no thought whatsoever.*

21 *"**But then, do you remember, <u>what return did you get</u> from the things of which you are now ashamed of?**"*

All you got was guilt and shame! The end of those things is not real life and true freedom, but death at the end of a path of self-destruction, <u>*and you know it*</u>*!*

(I am sure every single one of us have our own gory stories we can tell about that.)

22 *"**But now that you have been set free from sin and have become willing slaves of God, <u>the return you get is sanctification, and true freedom</u>, and its end, eternal life**"*

(...**<u>Life spent in real enjoyment and contentment forever</u> with God your true Father who loves you!**)

23 *"**For the wages of sin is death, but <u>the free gift of God</u>, given to all Mankind in Christ Jesus, our Lord, is eternal life.**"*

Chapter 6

"Go and Sin No More"

Listen, **if we want to reign in life,** I do believe that it is particularly vital that we must settle the fact that *even though we fell from our true identity* **and lived trapped in a false identity,** even though *we lived* **in a fallen state and fell away from truth,** even though **we lost our way in our thinking** and **got lost,** even though *we* **fell into deception and came under the influence of** the father of **lies, we must settle the fact that we (Mankind) <u>never actually</u> belonged to the Devil</u>!**

The Devil never *actually* was *our real Father,* he only kidnapped us, and assumed fatherhood over us.

The Devil only *influenced us and manipulated and controlled us,* but he never was our *true Father and* <u>we were never actually</u> *his children*.

The Devil is only the father of *lies and deception, nothing more!*

We must also settle the fact that we (Mankind) never <u>*actually*</u> had a sin-nature; *we merely <u>took on</u> a sin-nature.* Without this revelation, **without a clear understanding**

concerning this matter, *it is impossible for you to reign in life.*

I say again: **If you still hold to the teaching of a dual-nature or to a doctrine that tells you and tries to educate you and indoctrinate you that you have a sin-nature, that you were somehow born with it, *it will be impossible for you to reign in life!***

Listen; no one will be able to consistently resist temptation successfully *if they still cling to a dual-nature theory!*

Such a teaching, such a theory, such a philosophy *introduces and brings* **an inevitable weakness in our thinking and our belief-system,** *and therefore we are rendered almost powerless in our ability to overcome temptation.* **No one can reign in life that way!**

I know this revelation that you do not have a sin-nature, or even a dual-nature, will be truly hard for many of you theologians out there to swallow, *but the truth is we were custom designed to match the Divine-nature. The very image and likeness of God remained engraved in our inner man, even in spite of the Fall.* <u>We just lost sight of it, we lost the expression of it;</u> *we fell away from the full expression of it.* That is what the Fall of Man is all about!

Sin and death, was introduced through a lie. Sin and death, **like an outside force that**

comes in and invades the planet, _came into this world_ through that lie, through deception; through us swallowing that lie!

Sin and death, *this outside force,* came in and took us over, and it became a law within us and lorded over us!

It came into power, it reigned in our lives, it ruled us through ignorance and deception!

*"…being alienated from the life of God, **because of ignorance**…" Or more accurately, **through ignoring the truth** about God, which we, in our inner-man, **already knew to be true.***

Listen; we bear Father God's image and likeness, we come from Him. He is our origin; He is our Daddy, our true Father, the One who gave our spirits birth! *He formed us and fashioned us in our mother's womb and there He merely clothed us with flesh, but we are spirit-beings, we originate in God; we are way more than flesh.*

2 Corinthians 4:4 says that the enemy veils (blindfolds) the minds of those *who refuse to believe these things.* He veils (he blindfolds) their minds, *to keep them from seeing the light* ...to keep them from grasping the knowledge ...to keep them from gaining understanding into *the accurate truth* of the gospel which is: *The brightness of the **glory** of God* (The word is DOXA in the Greek.) ***The exact thought and accurate opinion of God***

concerning our true identity as it is revealed in the face of Christ Jesus ...as it is revealed in the incarnation and work of redemption, *just as your identity would be revealed to you when looking into a mirror!*

I say again: The enemy veils (blindfolds) the minds of those *who refuse to believe the gospel, from seeing the light of the gospel, **from seeing the glory of God; the exact thought and accurate opinion of God concerning us, as it was revealed in Christ.***

You will do well to go and read 2 Corinthians 4:6 and 2 Corinthians 3:18 for yourself. Read it slowly to yourself, until you get it, until the light comes on and you see for yourself what is actually being said by God, through Paul, there in those two scriptures!

*The enemy veils (blindfolds) the minds of those who refuse to believe the truth of the gospel, which tells them plainly that **the glory that was revealed in Christ is also in them**!*

That unbelief is the veil; it is the blindfold the enemy uses to keep people *from clearly seeing, from accurately understanding the truth of the gospel;* **from seeing with unveiled face that the glory of God revealed in Jesus Christ *is also in them*!**

Your true identity is revealed to you in the incarnation and work of redemption. Your true identity is revealed to you when you

are looking into the face of Christ, *as if you are looking into a mirror*!

Whom do you see when you are looking into a mirror?

You see yourself! You don't see someone else; ***you see yourself!***

The terrible thing about *doing window-shopping,* **as opposed to looking into a mirror,** is that it keeps you standing there, staring at something **without appropriating it.**

Why is this?

It is because; *in your thinking and in your mind it is **out of your reach.*** **You don't think you can have it,** *because you assume you cannot afford it.*

But you see, when it comes to the glory of God, when it comes to **the exact thought and accurate opinion of God concerning us,** *when it comes to that **true identity, YOUR true identity,** you do not have to try and afford it,* because **someone else has *already paid the price-tag,* and that item you are staring at, and thinking it will never be yours, has been given to you already as a gift!**

So stop doing window shopping, *put on **that which is custom made for you*** and discover that ***it does fit.*** **It's your exact size! God's truth about you measures and defines the exact dimensions of your being!**

You and that truth, the truth of the gospel, the truth about your original design and therefore true authentic identity, *are absolutely compatible,* **custom designed for each other!** It's **an exact fit!**

Put on the truth and stare** at **your true self <u>in the mirror</u> of Christ Jesus; in <u>the mirror</u> of the incarnation and work of redemption!

Go ahead, put on the truth and stare** at **your true self.

Do not just glance at your true self, stare for a while. Look deeply into that most liberating truth of the gospel!

Do not just glance and dismiss what you see, like you have done so many times before.

Do not just turn your back, and walk away, *forgetting again so easily what manner of man* **God reveals you to be in the mirror of His truth.**

Do you not realize that the Deceiver *needs your permission and disbelief, or unbelief,* to keep you ignorant and defeated?

That is why the apostle James says that *we only deceive ourselves when we look away from the word of truth.*

We don't deceive anyone else; **we only deceive ourselves!**

We deceive ourselves **when we look away from the gospel of our salvation and forget what manner of man <u>we are</u> in Him, by His doing.**

Do not allow yourself, *in your thinking,* to entertain any contradiction to the truth of redemption. **It will keep you in bondage to a fallen identity, a false identity, *an* alternative fulfillment, an alternative lifestyle, *when <u>in fact</u> you are a redeemed individual already!***

Let me ask you a question: If someone stole something, *at what point does that something ever legally become their property?* I mean, how long must they have that something in their possession *before it legally becomes theirs?*

The correct answer is: **NEVER!**

Yet the *"Church",* taken captive by the man-made Christian religion of today, by man-made religious beliefs, *have been themselves deceived for so many years!* **Religion has handed over ownership of Mankind to the father of lies.**

But the truth is: *"****The earth is the Lord's and the fullness thereof, the world and those who dwell therein!****"* - Psalm 24:1

It is quite interesting to discover that only two short chapters after Jesus said to the Pharisees that they are of their father the Devil, He quotes to those same Pharisees Psalm 8,

"I say you are all God's (God's property, God's family …you are all little gods, because) **you are all sons of the Most High!***"*

You can go read this encounter between Jesus and the Pharisees for yourself in John chapter 8 through 10.

You see, "they have forgotten the Quarry **they came out of** *and the Rock* **they were hewn from***."*

*"…the Rock **that begot them;***"

They forgot *"…**the God that gave them birth**."*

In Isaiah 49, God challenges the strongest bond in human relationships *because He wants to make a point.*

He asks, *"Can a mother forget her suckling child?"*

"As unlikely as that may seem;"

*"...even if that mother could forget her suckling child, **it is impossible for your Creator to forget you!***"

He says *"…**I have engraved you on the palm of My hand**."*

Luke 15 is such a clear and dynamic reference to how Jesus views *fallen Man, living in sin.*

He merely views them as *those who have lost their way.*

You see, *the original Owner remains persuaded* <u>**about the original identity and value**</u> of *the lost sheep, the lost coin, and the lost son!*

Listen; the Devil truly is **only *the father of lies.* He is not the father of Man;** *he has not fathered one human being.* **He has never been the father of anything or anyone and he cannot claim to have designed one cell in one body. He isn't anyone's father;** *he is only the father of deception, the father of lies!*

But you see, while I take the lie and I entertain it and believe it, *the lie takes hold of me, and sets up residence in me, like a parasite or a virus, and it enslaves me.*

The lie then *manifests itself in me, through me,* **just like a parasite** ...**just like a virus.**

And as we know from medical science: The virus never takes on the person. I mean, the characteristics of the virus are just that, it is the characteristics of the virus; *while the person remains the person.* **The virus merely manifests itself in the person**. Flu looks the same and manifests itself in the same way in any person, *no matter who the person is.*

And let me tell you… ha… ha… ha… when that snot-sickness lays hold of you, *it ain't pretty my friend!* It makes your life *downright miserable!* You see, **that thing, that virus, that bug is looking for a host.**

Now, it doesn't matter how sick a person is, *nor for how long he has been sick with the flu virus,* **never at any point does the symptom become the person.**

Listen; you can never become the flu. **You can get the flu and die from the flu, *but you cannot become the flu.***

No real doctor will walk into a room full of sick people and start slapping the guy who is coughing, and yell at him: *'Stop! This is your last cough!'*

No! Ha... ha... ha...

He knows how to distinguish the person *from the symptoms,* **and he knows how to treat the root of the problem *to make those symptoms go away.***

In the same way, God's accurate truth concerning your true identity; what is revealed there in Jesus' incarnation and work of redemption on your behalf, is *the antidote to the power of sin!*

You see, **if sin was and is *the fruit of deception,* then how can sin be a nature?**

Is deception a nature? *How can deception be a nature?* **Deception cannot be a nature.**

Deception is *the distortion* of truth.

Deception is *the fruit* of <u>believing a lie</u> or <u>preferring a lie</u> over the truth.

Deception by definition is not a nature; *it's <u>the absence</u> of accurate truth.*

Therefore sin cannot be a nature either, because **sin was and still is <u>the fruit of deception.</u>**

SIN, HAMARTIA *in the original language, is:* ***Missing the mark.*** It is **missing the mark <u>of accurate truth</u>!** *It is merely the fruit of ignorance, confusion, and deception!*

God is not the author of confusion, but of light, enlightenment, clarity, accurate truth, insight and revelation!

God's accurate truth is *the antidote,* **the cure to the power of sin!**

Jesus said, *"If you continue in my word, then you are my disciples indeed, and **you shall know the truth, and the truth shall make you free.**"* - John 8:32

Listen, Man's *descent into darkness,* Man's fall from *glory,* Man's falling away from God's *original thought,* Man's falling away from God's *accurate opinion of him,* Man's getting lost *when it comes to God's accurate estimation of his real worth,* **does not mean that Man's design was somehow flawed; that God** *somehow made a mistake in the process of bringing Man forth from within Himself.*

Man was and is God's workmanship; *the very offspring of God.* **But we fell away from that truth, our eyes were blinded and we were blindfolded by the father of lies and fell into deception. We no longer understood our true identity and purpose. We no longer understood where we really came from. We no longer understood our sonship. We no longer understood our true identity as children of God!**

Listen; we are **His image, His likeness!** *We are **Love's very own image and likeness!***

We merely became trapped in a natural dimension of life, **but that doesn't change who we really are!**

We became trapped in this natural dimension, in our natural existence, in our natural lives, in an alternate life, living as mere Men, but that doesn't change who we really are!

We lived as mere Men, trapped in a darkened understanding, trapped in the futility of our minds, being driven by destructive passions and ill-conceived ideas. We were ruled by a debased mind, by the misguided passions and lusts and addictions of a body *controlled by a deceived, ignorant, confused <u>mind</u>!* **But** *that doesn't change whom God sees us and* *knows us to be! It doesn't change who we really are!*

We became the very products of *that darkness* **in the hardening of our hearts towards original spirit truth, and spirit realities!** We lived an alternative lifestyle, *which is no viable alternative at all.* **We lived our lives *in self-destruct mode!* We lost track of, and remained ignorant *towards, the fact that we do not exist by accident.* But that doesn't change who we really are!**

Listen, I have news for you, good news! You are not here because your parents wanted you or didn't want you; *you are not here by accident!* You do not exist by accident; *you are not a mistake!*

God desired your existence, and brought you forth from within Himself, to be His companion for life! To be the object of His affection! God desires you! He desires reconciliation! He desires an intimate relationship with you! He wants to lavish His love upon you!

Psalm 139:13 & 14 says that **God formed us and fashioned us.** We are fearfully and wonderfully made! **He put us together in our mother's womb (our spirit-man),** *and there He clothed us with flesh,* **but <u>we</u> are more than flesh and blood.**

We are spirit beings, made in the image and likeness of God, who is Spirit you see.

But *instead of living by these realities, we became enslaved to* living a lesser life, *a lesser identity; a life we were not originally designed for.*

These forces of darkness *ruled us and enslaved us.* **It is called <u>the law of</u> *sin and death* - <u>separation from</u> our original design and purpose; *<u>missing the mark</u>* of our original design and purpose!**

Sin and death became *the dominating force, the governing reality, which ruled and governed our lives, both in thinking and in conduct!* **But to say that we now *actually had* a sin-nature, or *were born with* the Devil's own nature, is absolutely preposterous.**

It is not only an insult to us; it is <u>*an insult to our origin, to the design and workmanship of our Maker*</u>!

It is an insult to our very Origin, to God Himself, to our Father; our Daddy, *to His image and likeness we.* It's a direct insult to His very own design, to His person, *to His very being, from which we came!*

If the nature of sin was fallen Man's *actual* nature, then why would God bother to challenge fallen Man about sin?

I mean if Man *was left with no choice but to sin* because he *actually* had a fallen nature, why bother telling Cain to, *"watch out"* and that, *"...*
104

sin is at the door, **but you must master over it!"**

How cruel. How insensitive of God to dangle a proverbial carrot in front of a donkeys' nose then! I am saying **it would be unrighteous of God to expect something from a man** *who is totally incapable and unable to live up to what is being expected of him,* **especially being merely a helpless slave, a slave of sin,** having *actually* **a sin-nature.**

If Man after the fall had **an *actual* sin-nature**, *then what about Enoch "…***who walked with God** *and was no more* (couldn't be found on earth) **because God took him***..."?*

And what about Joseph, who ran away from Potiphar's wife **and refused to give into sin and lust?**

And what about so many other patriarchs **who lived for righteousness?**

What about the woman caught in the act of adultery or the others to whom Jesus said, *"***Go and sin no more.***"?*

I want you to notice that He didn't say, *'Go and try to sin* **a little less,***'* or *'***try to just not get caught the next time,** because God knows, you really can't help yourself, now can you!'*

Jesus wouldn't have said, *"***Go and sin no more,***"* **if they didn't have the ability to do it!**

The trouble started, and still does, *not in the nature, but in the mind* of Man. Man got lost *in his thinking* first, *in his way of looking at and reasoning about things.* **He got lost *in his knowledge,* he got lost in *the knowledge* of good and evil.** Man lost his way *in his reference of himself.* Man lost his way *in the way he saw himself,* **what he believed about himself and about God and about life and about the way it's supposed to work.**

No one can live *outside of* his own thinking, **outside of his own thought-life.** *We live within the boundaries of our thought-life,* **within the boundaries *of our mentality* about things, within the boundaries *of what we truly* believe!** *You live what you think and believe.* **What you *truly* think, what you *honestly believe* controls you.**

Man lost his way in his thinking, **in his mentality, in his beliefs!** *And his nature began to express it.*

"**As a man thinks in his heart, so is he.**" - Proverbs 23:7

A man's nature is what his thoughts are, **what his thinking is, what his mentality is; his actual beliefs.** *That is a man's nature, his tendencies, his particular bent!* As a man *thinks in his heart,* **in his private thought-life, so is he!**

Paul says,

*"**I am not embarrassed** …**I'm not ashamed <u>of this gospel</u>**"*

Hallelujah!

That means: *"…**In this gospel I am not embarrassed anymore; I'm not ashamed anymore! I am no longer embarrassed! Because this gospel is the power of God unto total salvation, unto wholeness, unto complete wholeness of being!**"*

Chapter 7

Faith and Power

*"...**the gospel is the power of God unto total salvation,** unto wholeness."*

*"...**this is the key to its power:** in this gospel **the righteousness (the true identity) that comes from God alone** is revealed..."*

(The original authentic nature is revealed! The life that comes from God alone is revealed in the gospel!)

*"...in the gospel, **the righteousness of God (God's own righteousness)** ...is revealed"*

(Not only His goodness, but His right-ness, **what right God has to say what He says about us, about the true nature of Man, about Man's true identity,** *about His claim upon Man as His own.* **That is exactly what** *"...<u>is revealed!</u>"* **in the gospel.**)

Romans 1:16, 17.

You see, ***God's reference of us, in eternity,* in Christ, revealed and reinforced in the incarnation and in the work of redemption, *is where accurate truth and accurate faith comes from.***

God is the author of *accurate truth*. God is the author of *accurate* Christian *faith*.

Romans 10:17,

*"**Faith comes** <u>**by hearing**</u> **the word**..."*

(...by hearing the RHEMA: The revealed word, the manifested word, the revelation of the word made flesh, the revelation of Christ; that revelation of original righteousness, of original identity, of our redemption).

Faith comes by *that* revelation; *accurate faith* comes by hearing *that <u>revelation</u>!*

In the life, death, and resurrection of Jesus Christ, God did something with Mankind, and for Mankind, that is simply immutable. That means *it is not subject or susceptible to change or variation in any form, quality, or nature whatsoever.* **It means that the success of what God accomplished remains *unchallenged and unaffected by anyone's unbelief.***

In Jesus, *God removed every obstacle and hindrance that stood between Himself and Man!*

Every obstacle and hindrance *that stood against the restoration and manifestation of Man's original design and purpose* was removed in Jesus Christ! These things He did for us, *whether we are aware of it or not, whether we believe it or not!*

In His death _we_ died. In His resurrection _we_ were elevated to a new position of _blameless innocence_ before God.

These things do not become true when you believe them; they remain eternally true, _even if you are unaware of them._

They're true _even if no one believes it_!

_**What is eternally true about Man because of Jesus,** **the truth about Man and God and the work of redemption, _would still remain true even if no one would believe it_!**_

Romans 3:3,

"What if some did not believe?"

"Will their lack of faith nullify God's faithfulness (God's faith)?"

"**No, not at all!**"

Now, listen carefully now: **Even though the truth remains truth _no matter what I believe, it does not cancel out the fact that I still need to believe it_.**

My faith matters _in every way_!

**Why?**

_**Because I only experience the benefit of truth _as I embrace it_!**_

The truth simply has no value to us, individually, to you as an individual, *if it is not combined with faith.*

You see; *faith is so much more* than correct information ...just as much as falling in love *is worth so much more to you* than *just knowing the facts* about another person.

<u>Faith is from the heart</u>; **it is so much more than just a head thing, *it's a heart thing!***

Faith doesn't come through merely knowing all the facts. Faith is not just inspired by truth; *faith is love inspired!* Faith only works through love! - Galatians 5:6

I can still remember the first time I met my wife, Carmen. I did not even know how to spell her name correctly. I didn't even know her last name, I didn't know her date of birth, or her background, and I have never told her this, but seeing her made my heart respond with a, 'WOW!'

Not knowing those other things about her *did not stop my heart from responding with a 'WOW!'*

When a beautiful landscape suddenly appears before you, ***don't you instinctively, instantly respond with appreciation,*** without needing all the facts and figures?

Hey listen, **faith is such a gift from God, *it's an instinctive, instant, response when encountering God.***

Whenever He reveals Himself, even in these words you are reading right now, ***your heart automatically responds with awe and adoration.***

Seeing what He sees *causes us to believe what He believes* **...Unless of course you have trained yourself so well in cynicism that your brain immediately kicks in and wants to disqualify what you are hearing in some way.**

When it comes to the gospel, however, you will find it difficult to simply dismiss and summarily disqualify what your heart already knows to be true!

I'm so glad that neither Jesus nor Paul ever wrote a *'statement of faith'*. They knew that the love and adoration and passion they had *in response to the beauty of the Father* **in the light of the gospel, could never be reduced to a mere doctrine, or a set of principles neatly categorized.**

Listen; all we could ever hope to express is ***a mere introduction*** *to the fullness we enjoy, an open invitation* for others **to see what we see.** *"…for we can do nothing against the truth,* ***only for the truth****."*

I say again: We, you or I, **can do nothing against the truth,** *but we can do something for it.*

Just think about that! We can allow it to have its full effect in us and through us. We can draw the maximum value and benefit from it as we combine it with faith, **allowing God to persuade us <u>fully</u>** *as He is Himself persuaded!*

When we are dealing with the gospel, *we are dealing with the faith of God;* **we are dealing with** *the very power of God!* *We are not dealing with our best interpretation, with our best commentary, with our best guess.* **We are dealing with** *the power of God!*

When we tap into the faith of God *we tap into the greatest force in the universe,* **the very force that makes the universe operate!** *We are tapping into the breath of God* **that holds the galaxies in place!** *We are tapping into the very power of God!*

I am not writing this book to try and have a little debate with you on some differing Scriptural interpretations. No, I am writing this book **for one reason only: To allow the Spirit of God, the Spirit of truth,** *to quicken your understanding,* **so that in that quickening** *you too, may understand God's calculation and conclusion* **concerning Jesus Christ and His work of redemption,** *and really concerning you,* **revealed in the gospel,**

revealed in God's reference, in God's faith *concerning us, concerning what was achieved on our behalf.*

You see; if I were to try and preach to you *a gospel that does not reveal these things,* <u>**I would not even be touching the power of God**</u>**.**

I mentioned earlier that Paul said, *"I am not ashamed to preach the gospel,* **for it is the very power of God,** <u>**unto salvation**</u> **(unto wholeness of being)***, for everyone who believes ...for in it the righteousness of God is revealed. From faith to faith* **(God's faith inspiring our faith***)"*

The power of God is the righteousness of God revealed in the gospel. It's *God's faith inspiring our faith.*

What right did God have, for instance, to say *this* to Abram?

'From now on I am calling you a father; and not just the father of the Jews, but also the father of many nations (…of all the nations)'

What right did God have to say to him, *'I'm going to change your name?'* What was God's righteousness, His *right?*

His ownership and His ability to say it and make it happen!

Now, what was Abram's righteousness? I mean *how was Abram able to experience the power of God?* **Abram just yielded to God's righteousness,** *to God's right.*

It's that simple!

He said, *'God,* **You're** *right about me!'* And Abram didn't just say it, he meant it, *he believed it.* He made it so ME, so personal, that the next time he introduced himself to somebody he introduced himself as the new creation God said he was. He said, *'Hello, I'm Abraham, the father of many nations.'* I mean, his very next conversation, after his encounter with God, was, *'Oh, so by the way, I've had a name change! I am no longer Abram, I am now Abraham."*

Faith came alive in him!

***Through what he heard* faith came alive in him!**

He was quickened in his spirit to *believe*! ***And because he believed, because he was quickened by the word, by the Spirit of Truth, he was able to respond to God and partake of God's power.***

I want you to see that that is the most powerful thing about faith: FAITH is not an argument that you can academically consent to, and say, *'Okay, yeah, that makes sense.'* **No, faith is so much more.** *Faith is a download of the power of God in your spirit.*

The wonderful thing is, because you are human, *you are faith compatible.*

The minute you turn your cell-phone on, *it works!* I mean, the minute they put that little sim-card into it, *it works.* **It is sim-card compatible.**

Can you imagine all the work and technology that goes into that little cell phone to give it all the capacity it needs to receive text messages and make phone calls, *and who knows what else these days?* **All it needs is** *that little initial ping, that quickening,* **from the sim-card, and off you go,** *making phone calls, and enjoying all it offers you!*

Paul prayed that <u>we</u>, **YOU included, may grasp the power of God that He worked in Christ's death** <u>*on humanity's behalf*</u>.

...and then by that same power He raised Him from the dead <u>*to convince us of that reality*</u>*!*

That is why I wrote this book. I see on a daily basis so many people in trouble **and I have been given the solution–correction–***we* **have been given the solution,** *in Christ Jesus.* **We have been given** *the cure,* **the answer, in the form of a pill,** *the gospel. It's the power of God* **unto salvation! It's the power of God unto freedom from the power of sin!** *It's the power of God* **unto restoration; unto wholeness of being, unto**

fullness of life ...**it's a full restoration unto** *the way life was meant to be lived!*

By grace, *by the power of God*, through the gospel, by *faith*, by *believing* the gospel, <u>the power of God is released to us</u>.

And we, <u>by that power, are indeed ruling and reigning in life</u>! **Our faith in the success of Jesus' work of redemption** *releases the power of God in our lives!*

Now, let us take one more look at that exceedingly sufficient grace in the heart of God *that is towards us* and let's look at *what it did for us* in Jesus Christ's work of redemption.

Chapter 8

The Work of Redemption

Ephesians 1:2-23,

2 *"**Grace to you** (everything that God has done in Christ on our behalf – it belongs to you,) **and peace** (the fruit of what grace accomplished for you – it is yours – as a gift) **from God our Father and the Lord Jesus Christ**."*

3 *"Blessed be the God and Father of our Lord Jesus Christ, **who has blessed us**, in Christ, with every spiritual blessing in the heavenly realm (…in the spirit realm …in the unseen realm of spirit reality),"*

4 *"…even as **He chose us** in Him (in Himself …in Christ, He associated us in Himself and in Christ), before the foundation (before the CATABALO; before the fall) of the world, that we should **be**, holy and blameless before Him."*

O the wonderment (*...is that even a word? Ha... ha... ha...*) that **He wanted us,** that **He chose us. He desired us! He favored us! He liked us! We are His choice!**

It is exactly <u>that</u> reality **which wins our hearts over and makes us exclusively His.**

5 *"He destined us **in love** to be His sons through Jesus Christ, according to the purpose of His will,"*

6 *"to the praise of **His glorious grace**, <u>which He freely bestowed on us</u> in the Beloved."*

7 *"In Him **we have redemption**, through His blood,* (this includes) *the forgiveness of our trespasses, **according to the riches of His grace**"*

8 *"…<u>**which He lavished upon us**</u>."*

9 *"For **He has made known to us**, in all wisdom and insight, the mystery of **His desire**, according to His purpose **which He set forth** in Christ"*

10 *"as a plan, <u>for the fullness of time</u>, **to unite all things in Him**, things in heaven and things on earth."*

His purpose was to bring God and us back together, to bring us and our original design back together, and to bring us into unity and true friendship with each other. *This was His plan all along.*

11 *"In Him, according to the purpose of Him* (God) *who accomplishes all things according to the counsel of His will,"*

12 *"we, who trusted* (believed …put our faith) *in Christ* (in His work of redemption), *have*

been destined and appointed **to live for the praise of His glory***."*

13 *"In Him,* **you also, who have heard the word of truth, the gospel of your salvation, and have believed in Him, were sealed with the promised Holy Spirit***,"*

14 *"…****Who is Himself the full guarantee of our inheritance, so that we may acquire possession of it*** (**here in this life, amen,** but we will also inherit a resurrected body like His one day, amen), *to the praise of His glory."*

15 *"For this reason, because I have heard of your faith in the Lord Jesus and of your love towards all the saints,"*

16 *"I do not cease to give thanks for you, but I also still remember you in my prayers,"*

17 *"that the God of our Lord Jesus Christ, the father of glory,* **may give you a spirit of wisdom and revelation in the knowledge of Him** (in the gospel)*,"*

18 *"***having the eyes of your hearts enlightened** (through that very gospel)**,** *that you may know what is the hope to which He has called you; what are the riches of His glorious inheritance in the saints* (***in you,*** in other words)*,"*

19 *"****and what is the immeasurable greatness of His power in us who believe,*** *according to the working of His great might"*

20 *"**which He accomplished** in Christ when He raised Him from the dead and made Him sit in and as His right hand in the heavenly realm,* (in spirit dimension, in the unseen realm of spirit reality)*,"*

21 *"**far above all rule and authority and power and dominion**, and above every name that is named, not only in this present age, but also in that which is to come;"*

22 *"and He has put all things under His feet and has made Him the head over all things, **for the sake of the church**, (His* EKKLESIA*)"*

23 *"which is His body* (of believers ...His very own expression of His work of redemption on earth, and of His nature, of His image and likeness, and of His person,) ***the fullness of Him*** *who fills all in all."*

Ephesians 2:1-10, makes expounds on that and makes it plain,

1 *"And **you** **he made alive**, when you were dead through the trespasses; through the sins* (through missing the mark)*"*

2 *"**in those sins** (in that **missing of the mark**) **you once walked**, following the course of this world, following blindly the prince of the power of the air, the spirit that is even now at work in the sons of disobedience* (still sons of God, but clueless and faithless and therefore in violation of the truth [disobedient])*."*

3 *"Among these* **we all <u>once</u> lived** *<u>in the passions of the flesh</u>,* **following the desires of mind and body, <u>and so</u>** (and therefore, as a result, we) **were by nature children of wrath.**

We were still children, but we were clueless and faithless and therefore in violation of the truth [disobedient children]. We were hostile children, full of frustrations and attitudes and anger. We were resentful and bitter, full of self-centeredness and hatred towards ourselves and others. We were hate-full and deserving of the disappointment and displeasure of others and so we thought we were deserving of those things from God also*;*

*"…***just like the rest of Mankind***."*

4 *"***BUT GOD***, who is rich in mercy,* **out of the great love with which He loved us***,"*

5 *"even when we were dead* (separated from God in our minds, alienated from the life of God in our experience) *through our trespasses,*

(...even though we thought we were deserving of this death, and for all intents and purposes, naturally thinking, should have been deserving of this death, **YET**)

*"***He made us alive together with Christ (by grace you have been saved)***"*

6 *"...**and raised us up with Him**, and made us sit with Him* **(in a place of authority)** *in the heavenly realm,* (in the realm of spirit reality), *in Christ Jesus,"*

7 *"that in the coming ages* (from now, throughout all time, towards all Men, in all generations yet to come) **He might <u>show</u> the immeasurable riches of His grace, in His fondness for us, and in His kindness revealed and exercised towards us in Christ Jesus."*

8 *"**For by grace you have been saved, through** (God's) **faith; and this** (this work of redemption) **is not your own doing, it is the gift of God**"*

9 *"not because of* (our) *works, lest any man* (any person) *should boast."*

10 *"**For we are His workmanship,*** (new creations if you will) *created* (there) *in Christ Jesus* **(in His work of redemption)** *for good works, which God prepared beforehand that we should walk in them."*

God planned this for Man. God planned for Man to be His companions, to be His co-rulers, to express His workmanship. Even before time began He desired this for Man, and so He reaffirmed this and restored us to it in Christ Jesus.

This is what the new creation and what GRACE is all about!

Colossians 2:11-15 says that,

11 *"In Him,* (Jesus – in His work of redemption) *you were circumcised with a circumcision made without human hands,* **by the putting off of the body of flesh, in the circumcision of Christ** (in the death of Christ)*;"*

12 *"and you were buried with Him,* (in being associated with Him in His death) *in immersion* (you are in Christ, associated in His death **by God's doing,** 1 Corinthians 1:30 and 2 Corinthians 5:14-21, God put you in Christ's work of redemption), *in which you were also raised with Him, through faith,* (you were raised simultaneously) *in the working of God who raised Him from the dead."*

(*"He was raised because of our justification"* - Romans 4:25.

Listen; we were raised through God's faith – God believed in the success of the work of the cross. **That is what brought about the resurrection.** That's the only basis upon which we can believe *in the success of the work of redemption.* **Our faith is inspired by His faith; it is merely the by-product of His faith, a response to His faith**).

13 *"and you, who* **were** *dead* (to God, separated in your heart and mind, lost) *in trespasses and the uncircumcision of the flesh, yes you,* **God made alive together with Him (together with Jesus)***,"*

"...having (past tense) forgiven us all our trespasses (there on that cross)"

14 *"having canceled the bond that stood against us* (our guilt) *with its legal demands* (it demanded punishment)*; this* (guiltiness and therefore its punishment, its shame, its condemnation) *He set aside,* (by) *nailing it to the cross* (in that open display of His extravagant love for us)*."*

(He took the government of sin and death, those forces of darkness that stood against us and caused us to miss the mark in the first place, that ruled our minds and our lives and caused us to be guilty, **He took it and nailed it to the cross,** *in the very apparent demonstration of His love for us!* **He canceled its hold and its effect, as well as its legal consequences,** *when He demonstrated His love for us so clearly!*)

15 *"He disarmed the principalities and powers and made a public spectacle of them, triumphing over them in Him"*

All the forces of darkness suffered an embarrassing defeat. He nullified their power, and their claim upon our lives, when he demonstrated His tremendous love for us!

Now that is **GRACE** my friend! **What I have shared with you in this book is the LOVE of God; the POWER of grace,** *available to you!*

I have no dominion over your faith; *I am only a helper of your joy.*

Believing these things, embracing them and laying a hold of them are *up to you* **personally in your life as an individual. Each individual shall stand for himself face to face with the Lord and His truth.**

So in closing, let me leave you with these words of encouragement. It's something Jesus often said, *"***According to your faith <u>be</u> it unto you!***"*

I want to bring to your attention some places *where you can find some more resources* to help you grow in your understanding of the original blueprint Son's coming in the flesh as Jesus.

We all really do need to understand Father God's message to us in the Christ. We need to thoroughly comprehend His work of redemption and restoration of **OUR authentic design** and **OUR true spirit identity** and **our authority.**

I urge you to get yourself a copy of *"The Mirror Bible"* available online at: www.Amazon.com and several other book sellers.

If you want me or someone a part of our team to come to where you are, *anywhere in the world,* and give a talk or teach you and some of your friends *about the gospel message and redemption realities,* simply contact us on www.LivingWordIntl.com, or you can always find me on Facebook.

I pray that God may richly bless you in your life and that you would prosper and be in health, even as your soul prospers in enjoying *God's exceedingly sufficient grace.*

I know that your experience of God's love and of His greatness will only increase as you begin to enter into this new kind of faith-relationship with God, which **He** has brought you into; *a relationship of love and power!*

If your life has changed in some small way as a result of reading this book, *please write to me and let me know about it.* I would love to share your joy, *so that my joy in writing this book may be full!*

"For
I am not ashamed
of the gospel
of Christ,

for it is the power
of God

unto salvation,
for everyone who believes…

For in it
the righteousness of God;
(God's right;
what right God has
to say what He says

*about Man, now,
in the light
of redemption)*

*...that is what is revealed
in the gospel*

*...it is from
FAITH to faith
(God's FAITH
inspiring our faith);
as it is written,
'The just shall live by faith'
~Romans 1:16-17*

About the Author

Rudi & Carmen Louw together oversee: Living Word International.

They also travel and minister both locally and internationally.

Rudi was born and raised in the country of South Africa, while Carmen grew up in Cortland, New York.

They function in the ministry of reconciliation (2 Corinthians 5:18-21) and flow strongly with the Holy Spirit and His anointing to teach, preach, prophesy, heal, and whatever is needed to touch people's lives with the reality of God's love and power.

God has given them keen insight into what He has to say to Mankind in the work of redemption concerning the revelation and restoration of humanity's true identity.

Therefore they emphasize THE GOSPEL, IN CHRIST REALITIES, the GRACE of God, the WORD OF RIGHTEOUSNESS, *and all such eternal truths essential to salvation and living the CHRIST-LIFE.*

They have been granted this wisdom and revelation into the knowledge of God by the resurrected Spirit of Jesus Christ, *to establish and strengthen believers in the faith of God, and to activate them in ministering to others.*

Not only are people set free from the poison and bondage of sin, condemnation and all kinds of intimidation, (upheld, strengthened and reinforced by age old religious ideas born out of ignorance) **but many are brought into a closer more intimate relationship with Father God, as Daddy**, through accurate teaching and unveiling of the gospel message, prophetic words, healings and miracles.

Rudi & Carmen are closely knitted together with many other effective Christians, church fellowships, and groups of believers who share the same revelation and passion *to impart the truth of the gospel, and so* ***to impact and transform the world we live in with the LOVE and POWER of God.***

www.ingramcontent.com/pod-product-compliance
Lightning Source LLC
Chambersburg PA
CBHW071128090426
42736CB00012B/2049